Choose joy.
Donya

From
Guilt
to
Glory

The Journey of a Mother

Donya Russell

From Guilt to Glory
The Journey of a Mother

Printed in the USA

ISBN (Print): 978-0-9981105-0-9

ISBN (Kindle): 978-0-9981105-1-6

Library of Congress Control Number: 2016914876

Published by Donya Russell | The Woodlands, Texas

To Contact the Author:

www.donyarussell.com

Contents

⌘ ⌘ ⌘ ⌘ ⌘ ⌘ ⌘ ⌘ ⌘ ⌘ ⌘ ⌘

To my Husband, Randy

I ordered waffles and got "Honey" to boot! You are the most loving, giving, and compassionate man I have ever known. Your love and support mean the world to me. Thank you for putting up with my kind of crazy.

To my Noisemakers
(Past, Present, and Future)

I am honored to be able to love, nurture, and help propel you towards your destiny. I am so happy that God chose me to be a part of your lives. My love for you is unconditional and knows no limits. Thank you for making me the Mom, Momma, Mommy, Auntie, and Meme that I am today.

⌘ ⌘ ⌘ ⌘ ⌘ ⌘ ⌘ ⌘ ⌘ ⌘ ⌘ ⌘

From *Guilt* to *Glory*

Introduction

Their squeals and laughter are so loud that I am pretty sure the walls are shaking. I have tried several times to keep this joyous play contained within the confines of the back bedrooms, but to no avail. They are just wild and loud and happy. They are kids. This is what they do. There are three of them and the noise is exponential. I must remove myself for just a moment before my head explodes. As I head down the hall to steal some solace in my bedroom I hear, "Momma, where you going?"

"Crazy," I reply in a flippant sarcastic manner.

A second voice screams in excitement behind me, "Oh, can we go too?"

"Are you kidding, you three are driving me there." *Get it? Driving me crazy.* I crack myself up. Laughing at myself: one of the many joys of motherhood.

In my life I have had many career aspirations. I have wanted to be many things when I grew up, if I indeed decided to grow up. I have wanted to be a ballerina, fireman, nurse, doctor, lawyer, teacher, accountant, forensic scientist, microbiologist, and even sports commentator; just to name a few. Several of these things I have actually gone to school for. I have half degrees in many subjects. In all of this indecision regarding my life goals one thing has stood steadfast. I have always, without a doubt, wanted to be a mom. From being a little girl playing with dolls, to being a young teen starting to babysit, to being a newlywed setting up my new household, I have known that one day I would be someone's momma. So I would be a ballerina mom, a fireman mom, a nurse mom, a doctor mom, a lawyer mom, a teacher mom, an accountant mom, a forensic scientist mom, a microbiologist mom, or a sports commentator mom. No matter the profession I chose, I would be a mom.

As many little girls do, I had grand dreams about motherhood. I would have 5 kids. Yes, I said 5. I would be the best mom. I would be the mom that all kids wanted to have. I would be the caring, loving, hugging, kissing, singing mom. My babies would be so happy. My house would be so clean. My food would be so delicious and nutritious. Everything would be so perfect in shades of pink and yellow (my favorite colors as a child). Every day would be glorious. This is the motherhood I dreamed of. This is not the motherhood I got. Because that was a fantasy and this is the real world. Fantasies and the real world generally do not mix well. Now don't get upset. I am not saying not to dream or have fantasies of the life you would like to one day have. I am just saying that it's not realistic to think you can fight fires in a tutu while baking a cake. Understand?

It's not realistic to think you can fight fires in a tutu while baking a cake, understand?

Having the real world collide with your fantasy can get downright ugly. I mean it can get "somebody stashed a banana under the sofa and forgot it was there for a week and I found it while reaching under to find the baby's shoe" kind of ugly. Gross I know, but this is the real world after all. I was not the best mom. Like most new moms I had no idea what I was doing. I did care, love, hug, and kiss; but I recall a lot more crying than singing. My house was not clean and the end of the day when thinking about mealtime fast and easy was much more a priority than nutritious and delicious. The colors of my world were not always bright and shiny. Every day was not glorious, nor were the hills alive with the sound of music. I was overwhelmed most of the time and felt like a complete failure. I thought my babies (3 not 5) deserved so much better than what I was providing. Into my mind and heart crept self-doubt, confusion, frustration, and finally guilt. Guilt is a destructive emotion that pulls a person down. It has taken many years to climb out of that hole. To move from a place of drowning in low self-esteem to living in the full appreciation of who I am as a woman and mother has been quite the journey.

Journey: the act of traveling from one place to another; a trip, expedition, excursion, tour, trek, voyage, junket, or jaunt.

Life is filled with journeys. Some we enjoy more than others. Some journeys are easy and more enjoyable. The path feels straight and easy to navigate while there are others that are more strenuous. They contain lots of wrong turns and dead ends. The directions seem vague and unclear but the object of each journey is generally the same. The desired outcome is to actively move, to get to a desired destination. Sometimes as we journey through life, we don't actually know where we are going until we get there. We think the destination is one place when it is indeed some place entirely different. Such is the case for me with motherhood. Early on I felt like the destination was perfection. Through many ups, downs, wrong turns, dead ends, and reroutes I have realized that is not at all the case. We are not called as mothers to be perfect we are called to love, nurture, and be a blessing.

While navigating this frequently traveled road of motherhood I was introduced to this verse:

She is clothed with strength and dignity; she can laugh at the days to come. She speaks with wisdom, and faithful instruction is on her tongue. She watches over the affairs of her household and does not eat the bread of idleness. Her children arise and call her blessed; her husband also, and he praises her: "Many women do noble things, but you surpass them all."

—Proverbs 31:25-29 NIV

To me it was an outline of what God calls us to be as wives and mothers. For many years I would read these words and cry. I felt so far from the woman celebrated by these words. I felt so separated from the perfection I thought God required of me. Now, I read these words and rejoice. I smile and if there are any tears they are joyful ones. I know now that God is not asking for perfection. He already knows that we as mothers are fallible. However, He is here to guide us along the path. Allow me to share my experiences with you. The journey of a mother is a pretty bumpy ride, but I promise the final destination is well worth the bruises.

My Noisemakers

Chapter One

Let the Wild Ride Begin

Oh my goodness, I am so hungry. "Uncle, do you have any chips?" I ask as I wander into his kitchen. I am sure he can hear my stomach's violent complaints as I search for something to satisfy it. This deep intense feeling of genuine lack and emptiness was new to me. It just didn't seem reasonable. *And what on earth is that pungent stench radiating from this kitchen?* I quickly survey everything. The counter is spotless. There is not a dish in the sink. Nothing is out of place. The kitchen in the military home is immaculate.

Then what is that smell? Never mind, I need some food right now. Finally, soft white bread, sweet tangy sandwich spread, sliced ham, a slice of American cheese, thick ripe tomato slices, cold crisp lettuce and dill pickles. This is exactly what I needed. At last my hunger is

Waiting on Motherhood

satiated. Wait. Why is my stomach hurting again? Soon, I feel the saliva starting to fill my mouth. *No! No! No!* I quickly make my way into the bathroom, just in time. The delicious sandwich that I had just so greatly enjoyed has been ejected. Clutching my aching stomach, I stumble my way out of the bathroom and make my way back to the guest room where I have been staying. I find comfort in the cool room and even the low, cold air mattress is a welcome sight. I'll just take a nap. As I drift off to sleep, I realize that I have been sick like this for a couple of days. I am probably going to have to go to the doctor. I want to go home. I want my mom. At the very least, I want my own doctor. I don't want to have to go to a military doctor. For now, I will sleep. I will think about the rest tomorrow.

Through the sleepy haze I can hear my uncle calling my name. I struggle to focus on his voice. *What day is it? What is he saying? Husband?* Oh, my husband. I roll off the air mattress with a thud. My husband is on the phone. I giggle to myself as I make my way down the stairs to the phone. I have a husband. After 4 months, I am still not used to the fact that I had a husband. I am someone's wife. It still doesn't seem real. "Hey babe!" I giggled.

"Hey," he answered quickly, "Are you okay?"

"Um, yeah? Why are you so serious?" I replied, I don't think I had ever heard this tone from him. He almost sounded like an adult.

"Your uncle said you had been really sick. He said he keeps hearing you throw up."

Being the mature woman that I was I quickly turned in the direction of my uncle and stuck my tongue out at him (but of course his back was turned). *Tattle-tale*, I thought to myself. "Yes," I confessed, "I have been feeling kind of bad. I think I have some kind of stomach virus. I keep getting really hungry but when I eat I just puke it right back up."

"Did you call your mom?" he asked anxiously.

"No! I didn't call my mom! I am 19. I am a grown woman. I don't have to call my mom for everything."

I really wanted to call my mom. I really wanted to just go home. I didn't even want to be married anymore. I didn't want to be in North Carolina. I didn't want to have to go and find an apartment in South Carolina. I wanted my own room and my own bed.

"I'll call and go to the doctor tomorrow," I assure him. And after changing the subject and making small talk I ended the call. I make my way back upstairs and lay back down.

It took me another two days to navigate through the military medical system and make an appointment—everything was so foreign to me. Finally sitting in the waiting room flipping aimlessly through magazines I started to worry. *What if there is something really wrong? What if they start telling me things that I don't understand? What if God is punishing me for getting married without His permission?* My mind is racing. My heart is pounding. "Mrs. White? Donya White?"

By the time I hear what is being said, the nurse is practically yelling my name. *Oh, that's me.* I still don't recognize my own name. I start to giggle but the look on her face tells me she is clearly not amused. I jump up, clumsily gather my things, and rush towards her. I feel like I'm late for study hall. Her condescending glare confirms that I am. After a series of questions and tests. I have my answer. I am not dying. Not yet.

I make it back to my uncle's house and wait for my husband to call. When he finally calls it seems like he too has been stressed out all day. "Are you okay? Did they give you some medicine?" I can hear the concern in his voice. It is very sweet and makes me smile that he cares so much.

"No." I reply, "They did not give me any medicine."

"What? Why not?" His voice is so strained that I think he's about to cry; he's so worked up.

"Calm down. They didn't give me any medicine because the medicine that they would usually prescribe for something like this is not safe to give to pregnant people." I say very matter of fact.

Then I waited. I waited for the weight of what I just said to hit him. *Maybe I should have waited longer to tell him. Maybe this needed to be a more serious conversation. What if he's not excited? What if he is upset? What if he doesn't want to be a dad? I really want to go home. What am I going to tell my mom? How am I going to be someone's mom? What have we done? What is God thinking of me?*

"You're pregnant? Really?" he asked.

"Yes!" I say.

"This is so great," he stammers, "we are going to be parents! I can't believe it. This is the best day of my whole life!"

His genuine joy and excitement make me so happy. It momentarily erases all fear and doubt from my mind and heart. We are going to be parents. This really is the best day ever. Besides, we are married. This is what married people do. They have babies and make families. We are making a family.

And so it begins, I am on the road to motherhood.

⌘ ⌘ ⌘ ⌘ ⌘ ⌘ ⌘ ⌘ ⌘ ⌘ ⌘ ⌘

Allow me to back up a little. Let me give you some background. As I mentioned, at this point I was 19 years old. I had gotten married and was in the process of moving from a small town in Texas to join my husband (also 19 years old) who was in the Navy and stationed in Charleston, SC. I had grown up going to church with my Baptist mother and my Methodist paternal grandmother. My opinion of God was that He stood on high taking score, passing judgement, and keeping all infractions as a part of your permanent record. I knew that He could be good and could decide to bestow blessings on those who were favored. I was sure that those blessings were for only on those who had earned it. From all the sermons that I had heard it was pretty clear to me that only a very select few with the most pristine behavior could earn this favor.

To my knowledge, the words "pristine behavior" have never once been used to describe me. I knew that I was in the disobedient group referred to as sinners. So I spent most of life feeling very far from God's grace and separated from His presence. So much so that when I got married and the preacher said the words, "What God has put together ..." I was immediately consumed by an internal panic. *What if God didn't put this together? How would I even know if he did or didn't? What happens if he didn't? Will I go to hell? Are we going to get struck by lightning?* These were all real questions that popped into my head at that very moment. I was so confused. I felt sick. At one point I was pretty sure I was going to faint. So I did what any good Baptist/Methodist girl would do, I pulled myself together, said, "I do," and waited for the lightning bolt. I am not blaming either of my churches for this. I love those churches to this day. I still visit with family and have many fond memories at both. I am just saying that I did not gain much of an understanding of who God is and what He does. Now, let's get back to the journey.

⌘ ⌘ ⌘ ⌘ ⌘ ⌘ ⌘ ⌘ ⌘ ⌘ ⌘ ⌘

As the size of my belly increased so did the amount of my fear and doubt. I know this is common with expectant moms. After all, I was growing a tiny human inside me and that was just the beginning. My dream was becoming a reality. I was going to be someone's mom. Along the way in my religious training, I had managed to learn that babies were a gift from God. I knew that no matter how they got here that all babies were a blessing. Babies are perfect and innocent so therefore completely and wholly loved by God. They had never done anything to mess that up. So even if He was not pleased by me, He would still love and cherish my sweet baby. This fact, as I saw it, gave me extreme comfort. Now I had to figure out how not to mess up the life of this precious little bundle.

I decided that this would be a good time to start to pray. Not the sweet little memorized poems of childhood recited before meals and bedtime but real prayers to try to connect with God. I decided to throw myself upon the mercy of the court and ask God to forgive me. I would attempt to convince Him that I was now somehow worthy. My prayers probably sounded something like Shug Avery in the movie *The Color Purple*. I felt like I was chasing down my heavenly father telling him "I's married now Daddy!" ... trying to convince him that because I am married that I am now a respectable young woman worthy of His love. Okay. That may be a little dramatic, but really that is how I felt. I didn't feel like I was making any head way. I didn't feel anymore forgiven. I wasn't even sure what that would actually feel like.

> *I decided that this would be a good time to start to pray.*

Although at this point I still felt so desperate for God's love I had to let it go for a while. I couldn't focus on my needs. I had a baby coming. The baby's needs had to come first. I had things to do and cute stuff to buy. For the most part, I enjoyed being pregnant. Most of my days were happy days. I spent my time decorating and planning. I spent a lot of time cleaning. I even found the source of that smell. It was vinegar. I could smell the vinegar in everything. That strong, sour, pungent odor was not my friend. Anything with vinegar or a vinegar-like scent would practically burn the lining out of my nose. Catsup, mustard, pickles, salad dressing, coleslaw, hot sauce ... even sour dishtowels would make me instantly sick. I even spent a little time on bedrest after being diagnosed with preeclampsia, a condition marked by high blood pressure, excessive swelling, headaches, and extreme nausea and vomiting. Still these were just minor inconveniences on the trek to becoming a mom.

My husband and I had decided early in the pregnancy, as if there was ever any other option, that I would go back to Texas to have our baby so that I could be near my mom and other family members. He was scheduled to be deployed on a submarine leaving very near my due date, and being home alone with a brand new baby was not the least bit appealing to me. Being back at home with my mom made me feel safe. Even if I didn't know what I was doing, she did. She was practically an expert. An added bonus was that my mother was the Nursing Supervisor for Labor and Delivery at the local hospital where my baby would be born. Oh, and let me not forget to mention that she was also a Lamaze instructor and taught prepared childbirth classes. She was indeed an expert. In these classes we learned to focus and breathe through the pain. We learned all kinds of things to help us through labor. As expectant mothers, we learned to make a labor plan. Luckily we also learned that in reality, things don't always go according to our plans.

In my plan I would be sitting in the living room at mom's house watching TV. I would begin having contractions. My mother and I would time these contractions. I would walk around breathing like I had been taught until they were close enough to go to the hospital. Then I would grab my pre-packed bag and we would go to the hospital and have the baby. Yay baby! Oh, and all of this would happen on or very near my due date. This not how it happened. My original due date was July 25. At some point in my pregnancy the baby was measuring larger than they thought was appropriate for a baby at that particular stage so they moved my due date to July 15. Both dates came and went. I would occasionally have contractions but they were not frequent enough to time. It was July. I was in Texas. It was hot. I was miserable. Finally, in early August after realizing this baby had absolutely no intention of willingly leaving its cozy den, my doctor decided that it was time to induce labor. After nearly 48 hours of labor (yes, I really said 48 hours) my sweet baby boy arrived, all 9 pounds, 6 ounces, and 21 ¾ inches of him. I fell instantly in love with his not-so-little self. I was his and he was mine. I was now a mom.

⌘ ⌘ ⌘ ⌘ ⌘ ⌘ ⌘ ⌘ ⌘ ⌘ ⌘ ⌘

Thank you God for this blessing. Thank you for letting me have such a beautiful little gift. Maybe you do like me after all. I sure hope I can live up to your expectations.

⌘ ⌘ ⌘ ⌘ ⌘ ⌘ ⌘ ⌘ ⌘ ⌘ ⌘ ⌘

From *Guilt* to *Glory*

Chapter Two

The Next Stop

I hear nothing but the soft sweet snores of my chunky little 6-month old baby sleeping in the carrier in the seat beside me. I look at his peaceful, little round face. I lightly touch the tiny rolls and dimples of his little fat legs. He has grown so much in the last half year. Looking at him brings me so much joy. I know that there is a lot of activity going on around us, but I can't hear any of it. I am vaguely aware of the pale blue walls with some generic pictures hanging haphazardly on them, the metal and vinyl chairs arranged in groups of 3 and 4, and the messy piles of magazines that are always provided to help time pass a little more quickly in every medical office. *Wow! I am really hungry.* Deeply hungry. It doesn't make any sense that I should feel this hungry. Before it occurs to me to be concerned about this level of hunger, I hear the nurse call my name. I grab my baby in his carrier and the assortment of bags

The One Who Started it All

and trinkets that go along with him and follow the nurse into a consultation room. I'm thinking that this is just a formality and I am in a hurry to finish so that I can go and eat. *Good gracious, I am starving.* I am so hungry that it is nearly painful. I haven't felt hunger like this since …

"Well, Mrs. White, the test is positive. It appears that you are indeed pregnant." I look at the nurse and she is looking right back at me trying to judge my reaction. Disbelief. What she should have read on my face was disbelief and confusion.

"I don't think that's correct." I finally answer, "I already have a baby." I tell her and point to my sleeping baby. "I am actually only here to support my friend who needed to have a pregnancy test. They said that only patients were allowed in so I made an appointment too."

Now the nurse is the one who looks confused, "That may be so, but you took a pregnancy test and it is positive. You are pregnant." This time we both look over at my little love in the carrier. "So, Mrs. White, what do you plan to do?"

At this point I am light-headed and nauseous, either from the hunger or the news I have just received, but I manage to say, "I'm going to go and eat some lunch and then make a plan to have two babies. That's what I am going to do."

Pregnant? Again? I already have a baby. I'm not even sure what to do with this one on most days. What am I going to tell my husband? We are not ready for this. What am I going to tell my mom? I need to go lie down. Dear God, please help me.

Six months earlier when my son was born, my husband was able to be there for the birth but had to leave within days for deployment. I remained in Texas for two months to be near family and friends. We were with my mom and she was such a tremendous help. She was there to answer the massive amount of questions every new mom has. *How often should I nurse him? How do I know he's eating enough? How much should he sleep? How do I figure out why he's crying? Does he need a bath every day? What do you mean, I don't need to dress him in full outfits with coordinating socks and baby shoes every day?*

He was the first grandbaby so she was more than happy to hold him so that I could sleep when I needed to. This was great. At times I felt like I was still a little girl playing house. It didn't always seem real. It almost felt like someone would show up to take him back. I could imagine them saying "Okay Donya, playtime is over." Needless to say, that never happened. Now there would be someone new joining the play group.

⌘ ⌘ ⌘ ⌘ ⌘ ⌘ ⌘ ⌘ ⌘ ⌘ ⌘ ⌘

I am back in South Carolina and now navigating my way through motherhood on my own with a new baby on the way. My husband is deployed half of the year (a rotation of 3 months home and 3 months gone). I know it may sound crazy and that's because it is. Recent studies report that it takes the female body at least a year to recover after childbirth. So being pregnant so soon after giving birth presents certain challenges. For one, I was tired. My body was trying to repair itself, grow one baby, and provide nourishment for another. Also, my son started life bigger than average and kept up that pace for quite some time. By the time I was 4 months pregnant he already weighed just over 26 pounds. According to the restrictions from my doctor I could not lift over 15 pounds. Now, I am not a math genius but even I could see a problem with this.

With my husband out to sea so often we had to improvise. I would have to sit down, have the baby crawl to me and pull himself up. I would then have him step onto a small stool and climb onto the sofa then into what was left of my lap. From there I could stand up with baby in arms. Where there is a will, there is a way. I made my way through many of the unique challenges that being pregnant so soon after giving birth can present. Even still, much like the first time, this pregnancy went relatively well. I even avoided bedrest this time. I was so excited about the new life growing inside me. I couldn't wait to see its little face and count its little toes. I say "its" because we had decided not to find out the sex of the baby. We wanted to be surprised ... because two babies so close together is not a big enough surprise!

There was, however, one major obstacle to overcome. After talking to many other moms I now know that this issue was not unique to me. At the time it caused me a great deal of stress. It even kept me up at night. I loved my son so much. I was so consumed with all that he did and amazed by every new skill he conquered. I loved the smell of his hair, the feel of his skin, and look in his bright brown eyes. He was the most perfect of perfect babies. I felt that the new baby would be slighted. I could not imagine dividing the love that I have for this child to accommodate another. I had no idea how I would love another child as much as I loved this one. I wouldn't talk to anyone about it at the time because I felt so bad.

> *I could not imagine dividing the love that I have for this child to accommodate another.*

What kind of mom am I? Who has a baby that they know they won't love enough? What is wrong with me? My mom would never feel like this. My current baby boy doesn't even get to be a baby very long because there's a new one coming. I'm already a bad mom. I know God sees me. This is going to be yet another mark on my permanent record. Many days I was able to push these thoughts out of my head but they would come back from time to time. When the thoughts would come, the tears would come. My heart was breaking for this precious baby that I was carrying. Sure, it sounds crazy now but it was so real to me then.

⌘ ⌘ ⌘ ⌘ ⌘ ⌘ ⌘ ⌘ ⌘ ⌘ ⌘ ⌘

Fifteen months to the day after my son was born, I delivered a perfectly beautiful and healthy baby girl: 7 lbs. 8 oz. She was nothing short of glorious and with her was born a whole new set of love, just for her. It was as if my heart expanded just a little bit more. All of my tears and worry had been for nothing. There would be no need to share the love I had for her bother. No one would be slighted. I was overwhelmed with emotions and cried tears of relief. The moment they laid her in my arms I was smitten. She smiled at me and closed her eyes. From that moment on she has been my sunshine. Now I have two perfect babies and I am a mom times two.

My husband was fully deployed when my due date came. So once again, I had returned to Texas for the end of my pregnancy and to have the baby. I didn't mind at all. My heart was starting to believe that babies could not be born without my mother's presence—not my babies at least. Being home with my family was again a tremendous blessing. There were multiple people to keep my 15-month old son occupied while I took care of my baby girl. From the beginning I noticed that she was very different from her big brother. She preferred to be held. All. The. Time.

Still, transitioning from a mom of one to a mom of two seemed smooth at this point. Soon after we would return to South Carolina. I had always heard that it takes a village to raise a child. It didn't take me long to realize it is much easier to take care of two babies when your village is nearby. Eleven hundred miles of separation only allows for moral support, there is no hands-on help from that distance. It didn't take long for me to start to feel alone and in over my head.

Chapter Three

The Road Gets Rocky

"Momma! Momma!" I can hear my son calling from the next room. As the sunlight peeks in from behind the curtains I struggle to make the decision to start the day. "Momma! Baby crying!" Yes, the baby is crying. I can vaguely hear her. It mostly sound like she's playing in her crib. *Just a minute. I'll be there in just a minute.*

"Get this baby, Momma. Get this baby." Well he sure is pushy for an almost 2-year-old.

"I'm coming!" I yell down the hall toward their room. "Give Momma just a minute to wake up. Y'all are fine for just a minute."

"I get for you," he says.

Never a Dull Moment

"No you don't." I yell again, "Leave your sister alone. I'll be there in just a minute."

Well I guess my decision whether or not to get up right now has been made for me. I listen. They are quiet for now. Nothing seems amiss. "Alright Donya, you've stalled long enough," I mumble to myself. Just as I throw the covers back and reluctantly swing my legs over the side of the bed, he appears. I am startled beyond words. I cannot move for a moment. I reach my arms out slowly towards my son. He is standing before me with the biggest smile on his face and in his arms is his 6-month-old baby sister. He has his arms wrapped tightly around her chest. His little back is arched under her weight and he is holding on to her for dear life. Her arms are stretched out

24

before her reaching for me. She is clapping and happy. She too is smiling. I am horrified. *What the heck? How did he get her out? Please don't drop you sister on her head. What is going on here? Did he walk past the stairs holding her? I have lost complete control. Give me that baby!*

"Oh, thank you." I finally say as I gently lift the baby out of his arms.

"Baby crying," he says. "Get this baby. For you." He is just so proud of his little self.

"Yes, yes you did. Aren't you such a good helper? Now, let's not ever do that again." I examine the baby from head to toe. Not a scratch on her. She is just as happy as she can be. To this day, I still have no idea how he was able to get her out of the crib. This is one of life's great mysteries I suppose.

From that terrifying experience I learned to get up immediately upon hearing any noise from their room. Not that it always helped. Sometimes I would find them sitting on their bedroom floor quietly playing. Sometimes I would find them in the kitchen with the refrigerator wide open and eating butter. One thing was for sure, life with an infant and a toddler was never ever boring. It was at about this time that daily life started to get a little more difficult. Since I had returned from Texas I noticed that I would have these moments of overwhelming sadness. I assumed that I just missed my mom and family. There were other married couples on the boat and I had made friends with a few of the wives. However, when we moved back to Charleston after my daughter was born, we moved a little further away from the Navy base. The distance and the fact that we were all busy young mothers made it a little more difficult to connect. I was lonely. There were days that I would just lay down on the floor and let the kids play on and around me. There were other days that I just cried most of the day. I had no idea why, I just cried. Most days were not like either of these. Most days were normal. On the hard days, I would cry out to God, still not sure if he was listening.

⌘ ⌘ ⌘ ⌘ ⌘ ⌘ ⌘ ⌘ ⌘ ⌘ ⌘ ⌘

Oh dear God, do you hear me? I need you. I need you to help me! Please stop ignoring me. If you won't help me, please help my babies. I'm so sad. I'm so lonely. I can't do this. Please. You don't hear me.

⌘ ⌘ ⌘ ⌘ ⌘ ⌘ ⌘ ⌘ ⌘ ⌘ ⌘ ⌘

Even on the good days things were getting out of my control. My house was frequently a mess. Not a biohazard type mess, but an extremely cluttered type mess. There was paper and toys and clothes everywhere. My kids loved to tear paper. Newspaper, magazines, paper grocery bags, you name it was like confetti on my living room floor. It made them happy and I had no desire to clean it up. I would frequently start laundry and never finish so there were always overflowing laundry baskets and random piles of clean clothes all over the living room. Dishes were frequently left undone for days at a time. My husband was out to sea and the kids had no standard of cleanliness that needed to be met. Sometimes I was happy not to have friends so that way no one could drop by suddenly and witness how inept I was at keeping house. It would go on like this for weeks at a time. I couldn't figure out why this was happening. The hardest part was that I was a self-proclaimed neat freak. I preferred that things be very neat and tidy. Everything in my home had a specific place to be. I just wasn't putting it there. This mess caused me a great deal of stress and anxiety, but at the same time I was not able to force myself to do anything about it. Many days we just stayed inside with the curtains drawn. I was truly afraid that someone would witness my mess and perhaps call Child Protective Services. No, really, I had made it that big of a deal in my own head. I know now that just keeping an untidy house will not usually get your kids taken away but at the time, it was a real concern.

Finally my husband returned home from his deployment and I decided that I needed to do something. I needed to get out of the house. So I decided to enroll in college. Because when you are feeling completely overwhelmed it's always a good idea to add something else major, like college. *Sure, this will make it all better!*

I decided to take English, History, Biology, and Psychology. And as crazy as it may seem, it helped. It gave me such a sense of purpose. I was starting to feel good about myself again. I felt smart and important. Having to be at school at a certain time and needing to get the kids to a babysitter beforehand created a need for me to schedule and prioritize my time. I was able to get the kids up and dressed. I had to be dressed to go out in public. This meant that laundry had to be not only clean but put away and wrinkle free. The kids needed breakfast before we left home. So I cleaned the kitchen each evening to make morning meals easier. Since I had to do homework in the evening I had established a nighttime routine for baths and the kids even had a set bedtime each night. Life was getting better. I was happier and I distinctly remember some singing.

I actually managed to finish the first semester with a 3.8 grade point average. I was winning. Maybe I wasn't such a bad mom after all.

Just as school ended, I started to notice that my husband was becoming more and more distant. I realized that we had had a lot of changes in our lives over the last (also the first) couple of years of our marriage. We had two babies in just 15 months and because I had returned to Texas each time, we had also moved twice. I had stayed at home up until this point. Now I was in college. I felt that perhaps he was feeling a bit neglected but decided I would have to wait to be concerned about what was bothering him until the semester was over. *I mean, I am really busy. He can take care of himself for a little while. Right?* Wrong.

I am not sure of the exact timing but at some point things fell apart. One day I heard a knock on the door. When I opened it I saw a man standing there with a very pretty vase with a couple of red roses. "Ms. White?" I was so excited. Someone sent me flowers. It wasn't my birthday or anniversary. I don't think I had even been sent flowers for no reason. I signed for the delivery, closed the door, and quickly opened the card. They were from my husband. He had never sent me flowers for anything. Upon reading the card, my heart sank. It simply said, "We need to talk." That statement is never good. "I love you," would have been good. "You are beautiful," would have also been good. "We need to talk," was not good.

After avoiding the conversation as long as I could, we did finally talk. Well, he did. He told me that he was done. He was leaving. He said that things had gotten too complicated and that he was just not happy. This (our marriage) was no longer any fun. He said he loved me and cared about me but he was no longer in love with me. I was stunned. This had to be a joke, a really a bad, very unfunny joke. It was not a joke.

Just as I was building some self-esteem, just as I was starting to feel good about myself again, my husband decided to leave me. Neither of us knew what to do at this point. He didn't really have a plan. He just knew that he didn't want to be married. Since he would be leaving to go back out to sea soon we decided to leave things as they were. We would make decisions later. I tried so hard to act normal. I tried so hard to pretend that everything would work out. I tried but mostly I cried. I cried a lot. I was devastated. I went through so many scenarios in my mind of ways that I could have prevented this from happening. *I could have been a better housekeeper. I could have been a better mom. I could have not gained as much weight while I was pregnant. I could have lost the weight faster. I could have been more fun. I could have stayed at home and not gone back to college.* I think the thing that was the hardest for me to understand was that he had chosen to love me but now he was choosing not to. In my mind it was as simple as that.

> He had chosen to love me but now he was choosing not to.

I called my mom and cried. Then I cried some more. I couldn't even pray. My heart hurt and I just wanted to stop breathing. But I had babies. So I kept breathing and I even continued on with school. I decided that since he was deployed I could pretend that the whole breakup never happened. He had never really said those words to me. He had never actually decided to leave. This denial got me through the next couple of months. I think that perhaps he did the same thing because once he returned home from deployment we decided to reconcile.

Although we decided to try and make our marriage work the words he had spoken never left my heart. I felt like I was always on edge, waiting for him to change his mind again. I couldn't relax. I couldn't trust. I didn't know when he would tell me he was going to leave again ... which he did, several times.

4

Too Soon to Say Good-Bye

"H ey, where are you going?" he asked as I gathered my purse and keys.

"I'm just going to Piggy Wiggly to get some stuff for dinner." I answer absent-mindedly. I am so happy to be leaving the house without kids in tow that I am only half listening to this his questions.

"Can I go with you?" he pleads.

Really? Is he still pestering me to go to the store? My little brother is visiting from Texas. He is nearly 10 years younger than me and has always tried to get me to take him everywhere. I rarely did but for some reason this time it doesn't seem so bad. "Okay," I tell him. "You can come with me."

Our Last Photo With My Little Brother

"Alright!" he exclaims. He doesn't even try to contain his excitement. He jumps up and picks up his shoes. From what I recall he even beats me to the car. His smile is so big it's almost blinding. This is so funny to me. He is so silly, it's just the grocery store. Nonetheless, he loves his big sister and is just happy to be included. At the store we were totally silly and laughed about everything and nothing. I bought him junk food, ingredients to make his favorite cake, ice cream, and red soda. (Our mother was totally against red soda. As far as she was concerned it was just this side of evil). That is a trip to the store that I will remember forever. You'll understand better later.

My husband and I had decided to stay together, and things appeared like they had returned to normal. On the surface everything looked good. We were a happy, young military family. My sister had come to stay during the summer to help me with the kids and we all had so much fun together. We hosted parties and had lots of friends over … our house was the place to be! Also that summer, my mother gave my 12-year-old brother the option to go several places, including Disneyworld, but he chose to come and spend time with me and my family. He said he missed me and wanted to see me. I was amazed. I knew that as a 12-year-old my thoughts were rarely on spending time with family, but my little brother was just special like that. So one week before his birthday he came to visit.

Since his birthday was just a few days before my son's, we decided to have a dual celebration. He was turning 13 and my son was turning 2. Again, what teenage boy wants to share a birthday with a toddler? However, he seemed very excited by the idea. He loved his nephew. My mother had flown in to visit for the last weekend before everyone went back home. I was so happy to have my family there with me. We made a lemon pound cake, my brother's favorite. We had ice cream and festive party decorations, ready to have a great party. My brother started to feel bad and said he was having a lot of stomach pain. *Hmmm … maybe Mom was right. Maybe red soda is evil.* He wasn't able to eat much cake or ice cream. By the time they left the next day, he just didn't look well at all.

I got a call from my mom later the next week. My brother had been admitted to the hospital. He was now in excruciating pain and not doing very well. Although we had a large family and there were many people in Texas who were available to sit with him, he had requested me. He had asked that I come and be with him in the hospital since my mom had to go back to work, so I packed up and went back to Texas to sit with him.

When I arrived I could tell he was in a great deal of pain. I hated seeing him like this. After a few days they decided to put him in a medically induced coma because they could not control his pain. I sat by his bedside every day. The nurse said that he may be able to hear me so I read him stories. We had a mutual love of baseball so I shared the baseball stats for every team every day. I told him how much I loved him. I begged him to get well. I held his hand and I cried. I had taken him for granted and I was so sorry. Day after day, he remained in the coma.

I knew I would need to stay a little longer than initially anticipated and I decided that this would be the best time to return home and get my babies. I would go home and get them and be back before he woke up. I knew he would be so happy to see the kids. He loved them. By the time my plane landed in South Carolina the hospital staff had called all family members to return to the hospital immediately. He never came out of the coma. My brother began to feel sick on August 7 (his birthday) and he died on September 29 from complications of leukemia. I was numb but I cried out to God and for the first time in my life I felt like I heard him reply. He reassured me, "He is well." I missed my little brother so much, but I knew that he was okay. I knew that he was now healthy and whole. I knew that he was happy. I was thankful that he had not suffered for a long time. I knew that he was with Jesus. He was indeed well.

He never came out of the coma ... he died from complications of leukemia.

Even knowing these things, I was so sad. I cried all the time. I became crazy over protective of my children. I wouldn't let them out of my sight. Every sneeze and sniffle warranted a trip to the doctor's office. I didn't want my sister to return to college. I was afraid to leave my mom so I remained in Texas for several months after my brother's death. I had an irrational fear that if I left again that someone would die. I felt like I was going crazy.

⌘ ⌘ ⌘ ⌘ ⌘ ⌘ ⌘ ⌘ ⌘ ⌘ ⌘ ⌘

God why did you have to take my brother? He was just a kid. He didn't do anything wrong. Is it me? Are you punishing me? Are you going to take someone else? Please don't take my babies. I am so sorry for everything that I have done wrong. Please stop. Please don't take anyone else. I can't take this. Please.

⌘ ⌘ ⌘ ⌘ ⌘ ⌘ ⌘ ⌘ ⌘ ⌘ ⌘ ⌘

Eventually I moved back to South Carolina. My husband had once again been deployed so I was home alone with the kids. I had good days and bad days, happy days and sad days. To help brighten the mood on the sad days, I would take the kids outside. Much like me, they love being outside. They loved the sunshine. We had moved into a duplex and it had a nice yard and a private driveway so there was plenty of room for the kids to play and run. One day when we were playing outside my son kicked his ball under the neighbor's car. As I was retrieving the ball I noticed the dealer sticker on the bumper. The dealership was from a small town very close to the small town where I had grown up in Texas. *There is no way,* I thought to myself. This car has probably been bought and sold a thousand times. The person who owns it probably has no idea where this tiny little town is. No matter how I tried to talk myself out of it I was intrigued. For the next several days I watched out for my neighbor. She was young, maybe as young as I was (I was 21 by this time). I remember seeing her a week or so before. She was laughing with some other girls as they were leaving the house. She looked like someone I would have been friends with back home. I was trying to remember if she had an accent. I saw her come and go several times. She seemed friendly and happy. *This is crazy,* I thought to myself, *stop stalking your neighbor and just go and meet her. She's probably not going to bite you.*

About a week after noticing the sticker on her car I got up the courage to knock on her door. It was one of the best decisions of my life. It turned out that she was indeed from the small town shown on the dealer tag. We had grown up just 11 miles apart. We both laughed about the fact that we had lived so close to each other for so many years but had not met until now when we were 1,100 miles from home sharing a duplex. She too was a Navy wife. The sound of her accent reminded me of home. Her small town attitude was such a comfort to me. Her friendship was like a life preserver. We talked about how much we missed small town life. We even discovered that we knew some of the same people. At last I felt a connection with my new home state. It's funny to me that it came through my original home state. Even knowing that she could pop over at any time also made me keep my house a little neater. It wasn't perfect but it was better. Although she did not have any children yet she welcomed mine on any of our outings. It was so nice to have a shopping buddy, a friend. I could actually feel my heart starting to heal.

⌘ ⌘ ⌘ ⌘ ⌘ ⌘ ⌘ ⌘ ⌘ ⌘ ⌘ ⌘

Thank you, God, for my friend. I don't know what I did to deserve this or even if I deserve this, but thank You. Please tell my brother I love him and miss him. Please don't take my children. I'm so sorry for everything that I have done wrong. Please forgive me.

⌘ ⌘ ⌘ ⌘ ⌘ ⌘ ⌘ ⌘ ⌘ ⌘ ⌘ ⌘

Gradually the pain subsided a bit from the loss of my brother. I was able to function better on a daily basis. I really felt that God had given me time to bond with my brother before it was time for him to go home to his eternal home. We had grown so close during those few days. I learned so much about him. He was on the student counsel at his intermediate school. He played football (although he loved baseball the best). He had a girlfriend and he loved her smile. He had an awesome sense of humor. Although he was 13 years old, he was still just a kid. He was goofy and silly. I am still able to see the impression that he made of my son. I start to feel that maybe just maybe I was not completely lost to the love of God. I felt like maybe there was a chance to make amends. I know I heard someone somewhere say something about forgiveness. *Where is my Bible?*

Chapter Five

An Unexpected Stop

"Momma, momma!" She comes to me and throws her arms around my legs. I look down and see the tears streaming down her face.

"What's the matter, Punkin?" I ask as I pick her up. She's so tiny for her age.

"It's broken, Momma, it's just broken." She sobs. Now she has always been a bit dramatic so I glance around to what item has broken that has just ruined her whole world. I see nothing.

"What's broken, baby?" She sniffles and tries to catch her breath.

"This, Momma. This is broken." I look down again and see that she is pointing to her socks. The socks that I had just put on her little feet.

A Lover of All Things Ruffled

"Your socks?" I ask, a little bewildered. "Your socks are broken?" She is just over 2 years old, so sometimes we have a little breakdown in communication. I am just trying to clarify this morning's drama.

"Yes! Look at it! This socks is broken. I don't want it." She wails. Oh my, this is serious. At least it is to her.

"Calm down. Let me see them." I peel the socks off of her feet and examine them thoroughly. I am sure I will find a tiny hole or a pulled string or perhaps even a stain that I had missed when putting them on her. Nope. Nothing. I see nothing wrong with either of her socks. So, I attempt to put them back on her feet.

"NO!" she screams and proceeds to flail her legs around as if I am trying to trap her feet in flaming socks of some sort. "NO! It's broken and I don't want it!"

I attempt one more time to persuade her that there is nothing wrong with the socks. Then it occurs to me that I am seriously trying to reason with a 2-year-old. *Forget it. She can wear sandals.* Hopefully she will find nothing wrong with those. Days later, this same little precious one comes bounding in to the kitchen with a big smile on her face. "Look Momma. Look at my socks." She beams. "This socks not broken." I look down at her feet and she is lovingly touching her little socks and wiggling her toes. She looks absolutely delighted. I immediately notice the difference. These socks have ruffles. The faulty socks had no ruffles. They were broken, yucky, ugly, and therefore subpar. Yes, I spent the next couple of days sewing ruffles on all of her broken socks. I fixed them. Momma's little girly girl.

Things were going well. Life was pretty good. I had gone back to work. I had found a wonderful caregiver for my children. My marriage, although sometimes strained, seemed to be on an upswing. We had developed a core group of friends from the guys stationed on his submarine, some married and some single. My neighbor's husband was home from his deployment on an aircraft carrier so we even had another couple next door to add to our circle. We frequently hosted large family style barbeques and parties. I had decided to put off school for a little while and just focus on being a better wife and mother. I was getting better at finding the answers to life's daily challenges with two toddlers. There were few dark and difficult days. I was even starting think, *Yes, yes I think this is happy. I am happy.*

I have some friends who warn about getting comfortable. They warn that you should never be "off your guard." They say that this is when things will jump up and bite you on the bum. I am just not that person. I am a glass half full kind of person. I am always one to look on the bright side. I am not going to say those friends where right. I am just going to say that perhaps I should have been a bit more cautious. Perhaps I should have paid more attention to the signs being presented to me.

Several months into my newfound happiness and contentment, my husband once again expressed that he was unhappy. He said he felt that marriage was too difficult and he just didn't want to have to do it any longer. As was the case before, he told me this just a few days before he was to be deployed. Needless to say, I was devastated by his change of heart. I felt blind-sided. *How could this be? I was doing so well. The house was clean. The kids were clean. I cooked dinner. We were happy. I don't care what he said, we were all happy. How could this be hard for him? He didn't have to do much. I did everything. I took care of everyone including him. What was so difficult?* Now I was just angry. *Who exactly does he think he is? Why does he think he can just be off the hook that easy? Why does he just get to decide that he doesn't want to play anymore? Oh I have got news for him. He is not off the hook. He does not get to throw in the towel. He does not get to ride off into the sunset alone and pretend this marriage and family never happened. Not if I have anything to say about it.*

> *I was determined to change his mind and prove to him that he was wrong.*

So then, I was on a mission. I was determined to change his mind and prove to him that he was wrong. I know this all sounds completely insane but this is where I was at the time. In my mind I was fighting to save my family. My husband's timing (which had made me so angry before) was now going to work in my favor. I had three months to come up with a plan. I had three months to figure a way to convince him that he loved me and that he would be lost without me. Don't say it. I already know. You can't make someone love you if they don't. Trust me, I listened to the Bonnie Raitt song enough times that it is perfectly clear now. But at the time, I did not care.

As he prepared to leave to go out to sea, I was the perfectly dutiful wife. I made sure he had everything he needed. Uniforms? Check. Boots? Check. Socks? Skivvies? Check. Check. I even lovingly packed a special box of treats for him to have while he was gone. Since they were on a submarine there was very limited space so each sailor could only take a very limited number of items with them. Packing this box to contain all the things a guy would need and want while being away from home submerged in the ocean for 72 days was nothing short of an art form. I was very good at it. The single guys were often envious of the boxes of the married guys. My goal was to make him very happy to be one of the married guys. Did I mention I was on a mission?

When the ship is out to sea there can be very limited contact with the outside world. There were no chances for phone calls or emails but we did have the ability to send 8 short messages or familigrams as they were called. These messages could be no more than 40 words. They could not contain any bad news, anything shocking, and nothing risqué. Since they were transmitted from an office on shore to the control room on a submarine, many different people could and would read the messages before it arrived to your sailor. These messages were a very important part of my plan. I would take days to skillfully craft each message. I had to make sure that he missed us and was eager to return home to his family once his tour of duty had ended.

⌘ ⌘ ⌘ ⌘ ⌘ ⌘ ⌘ ⌘ ⌘ ⌘ ⌘ ⌘

Phase two of this mission was to work on myself. As many of us do, I had put on some extra weight during pregnancy and after. I didn't put as much effort and energy in to my appearance as I once had. Ok, it had seriously been years. Unless there was a special occasion or a date night, I was doing little to nothing to fix myself up. But, the kids were super cute so that should count for something. Right? Three months. I had three months to turn myself back into the bombshell he fell for back in high school. I cut my calories down as low as possible. For breakfast I ate a boiled egg and wheat toast. For lunch and dinner, I ate mostly baked chicken or grilled fish and salad. I would only drink water or Diet Coke. After getting home from work, picking up kids, getting them fed and bathed, and down to bed, I worked out for hours. I worked out every single day. There was no time to take a break, I was on a mission. It worked. I lost a lot of weight. He obviously did not know who he was dealing with. *Ha. Leave me? No way. I am smoking hot!*

You can go ahead and say whatever it is that you are thinking. I already know. It will be nothing that I have not said to myself thinking back on this time in my life. However, at the time I thought I was succeeding and I was on target to achieve my mission.

With just days left until his return, I began to select my wardrobe. The outfit that I wore to see him once they returned would be crucial. I chose a lovely floral fitted sundress to show off my new and improved figure. I looked like the perfect southern belle of a wife that I was (insert eyelash flutter here). There was no way that he would be able to resist. When the day came to meet the boat, I stood on the dock with all the other wives and girlfriends waiting to greet our men returning from sea. I had already sent him a message that I would be there so he knew to expect me. The look on his face when he finally spotted me in the crowd told me that my mission was a total success. He said he was wrong. He was sorry. He didn't want to break up. He does want to be married. He said he was just confused. I chose to believe him. After all he said exactly what I had wanted him to say and I got to keep my family intact.

⌘ ⌘ ⌘ ⌘ ⌘ ⌘ ⌘ ⌘ ⌘ ⌘ ⌘ ⌘

We reconciled, but it was very short lived. It lasted less than a month—such a short period of time most of our friends and family did not know that we had gotten back together. You can't make someone love you if they don't. You can't make his heart feel something it won't. I was once again heartbroken. I felt like a failure. I had done everything that I knew to do and it didn't work. I was once again so sad. I was so tired. It was all I could do the drag myself out of bed and function. Sad I understood, but it just didn't make sense to be this tired. Then all

> *I had done everything I knew to do and it didn't work.*

of a sudden I felt it. I felt that deep intense painful hunger. My body needed fuel and it needed it immediately. I had only felt this type of hunger two other times in my life. *Oh no. No. No. No. This cannot be. Not right now. God, You are not funny.* I loaded up my babies in the car and headed for the nearest pharmacy. A couple of hours and about six tests later it was confirmed. I was pregnant. I sat in the midst of the six little sticks with the six blue plus signs on them and I cried. I cried for a long time. Now, let me clarify. I was never once saddened by my pregnancy itself. I was upset about the timing and the circumstances.

The first person I told was my mom. I called her and I cried some more. I'm glad I did. She made me laugh. When she asked why I was so upset I explained that my husband and I were still separated and that this was not a good time to be pregnant. She replied as only my mom could, "Well, Donya, obviously you were not quite as separated as you had intended." *Touché mom. Touché.*

My husband received orders to be stationed in San Diego, California. The kids, my belly, and I packed up and moved back to Texas. In January of the following year, I delivered a perfectly beautiful baby girl. Like her brother and sister before her, she was born with a head full of hair and big brown eyes. I took one look at her and was instantly reassured that she was indeed a gift from God. Her father was there for her birth and shortly thereafter he moved to San Diego without us.

Chapter Six

Around a Dark Corner

*B*oom, boom, boom … here she comes barreling down the hall, this radiant little ball of sunshine and energy. She bursts into the room, her face and hands still sticky with the peanut butter and jelly from her lunch. "Momma," she shouts, "Need some milk!"

Does this sweet baby not know that I am just too tired for this? Does she not know that I just used the last of my energy to even make the lunch that is now smeared all over her little brown face? No, no she doesn't. Nor does she care. She is 3 years old and just wants a drink to go with her lunch. So, with all the energy I can muster, I pull myself out the heavy darkness and make my way towards the kitchen.

I am greeted by her big brother, "Mommy! Yay, you're up!" he cheers. It seems that even my 4-year-old knows what an accomplishment

They Kept Me Going

this is. I look around and survey the damage that has been done while I laid in the dark in the bedroom and let a 3 and 4-year-old run free for an hour.

What is wrong with me? Why can't I be the mom I am supposed to be? My poor babies. They deserve so much more. Oh, yes, milk. I am getting milk. With a heavy sigh, I walk into the disaster zone that serves as our kitchen. I can't even talk about that.

My life went on like this for days, weeks, and months. My main goal was to get my babies through the day. I managed to make sure they ate three meals and two snacks. I was careful to make sure they were bathed on most days and that they were neatly dressed each morning. Completing these simple tasks each day represented victory to me. They became the things that got me through each day. So much so that the carefully prepared to do lists became my road map from the children's wake up time to their bedtime:

- 8:00 am – Wash faces and brush teeth

- 8:30 am – Big kids breakfast, nurse the baby

- 9:00 am – Everyone dressed

And so on, and so on. After bedtime, however, I was lost. They were all sleeping. They didn't need much from me for a little while. There was just too much time to think, too much time to lay down and cry. I would make promises to myself. *Okay, today was a bad day but tomorrow, I promise I will do better. Tomorrow I will wash all the dishes and fold all the clothes. Tomorrow I will smile and laugh and be happy. Tomorrow I will be a real mom. Tomorrow I will be the mom God wants me to be. I know He must be so horribly disappointed in me. Why would He give these beautiful babies a mom like me? They deserve so much more.*

⌘ ⌘ ⌘ ⌘ ⌘ ⌘ ⌘ ⌘ ⌘ ⌘ ⌘ ⌘

God, please help me. Do You hear me?

⌘ ⌘ ⌘ ⌘ ⌘ ⌘ ⌘ ⌘ ⌘ ⌘ ⌘ ⌘

By this time, my friends and family were not sure what to do to help me. I felt that my mom thought I was lazy and unmotivated. My friends had their own lives and I think the constant darkness that surrounded me frightened them. My husband had reported for shore duty in California and I wasn't sure that we would ever be joining him. At this point we rarely talked to each other. I felt so isolated and alone. I remember thinking that I just didn't want to wake up but I couldn't bring myself to ask God to take me. My kids deserve better than that. Besides, as far as I could feel, God didn't really like me anyway. Why would He? I was a disgrace. I knew I needed to get some help. There was no way that I could continue on like this. But, I did. I didn't want to talk to anyone about what I was feeling. They were my own feelings and they scared me. How could I possibly help someone else understand what I was feeling?

I found comfort where I could, in food. I would eat. I would eat constantly. I found myself cooking twice as much food as we needed. While I was cooking I would tell myself that I was cooking ahead. I would try to convince myself that I would be able to freeze the leftover food for another day. That never happened. After the kids were down for the night I would go back into the kitchen and eat the remaining food. All of it. I would watch TV and eat. I would cry and eat. I would sometimes even clean and eat. I would eat to the point that I was miserable. I remember asking myself, *How do people consider this comforting? There is nothing comfortable about it.* Sometimes it felt more like punishment. I did it anyway. I had so much shame that I withdrew even further from my friends and family. I wouldn't even eat in front of my kids because I thought even they would judge me. It was crazy. I would buy food and hide it so they wouldn't know to ask for it. This way I could eat it while they were

> *I had so much shame that I withdrew even further from my friends and family.*

sleeping and they would never know. I was gaining weight rapidly. I didn't care. I had no one to impress. My kids would love me anyway. My mom outfit consisted of sweat pants and an oversized t-shirt, both of which could cover a multitude of sins.

Family members were starting to comment on my weight gain. My mom would gently ask if I was okay. She would mention that she noticed that I had put on a few pounds. My extended family is far from gentle and tactful. They would just come out and say it, "Girl, what is really going on? You just getting big and fat." "You better do something with yourself. You will never get that man back like that." Well, there you have it. I am now big and fat. I am big and fat and sad and pitiful. I'm going to go home and eat some cookies. Now that my weight gain had been pointed out to me, my extreme bingeing was followed by purging. I would eat until I couldn't eat anymore, then I would just make myself throw it all up. That way, there would be no evidence of what I had done. I continued on like this for months. When I noticed that I was starting to throw up blood I figured that I was damaging my esophagus so I stopped. I just stopped. I have no explanation for how or why. I just couldn't do it anymore but I still cried. I had no other outlet for the pain I felt so I just cried.

⌘ ⌘ ⌘ ⌘ ⌘ ⌘ ⌘ ⌘ ⌘ ⌘ ⌘ ⌘

After a long while, my husband began to call. He was lonely. He was sorry. He was wrong. He missed his family. He was on shore duty now. He would be able to help with the kids more. Things would be different. He promised. He said I would love San Diego. The kids would thrive there. We could be a family. Wait? Now he was trying to convince me? I was not the one who left. I was still angry. *You can't just throw away your family and then decide to change your mind,* I thought. Well, maybe you could. *Is this not what you wanted?* I pondered. Besides, the alternative was to stay right where I was. *Kids are better off with two parents and even a little help would be good. California is sunny. I like the sun. But wait, I had gained so much weight. I needed to start exercising. I needed to stop eating. I needed to postpone this reunion until I could get myself together. Oh forget it. When you discard your family you just get whatever you get when you pick them back up. Ha. He deserved to have a fat wife for a while.*

I packed up the kids and moved to San Diego with my husband. He was so excited to see all of us. I think he really did miss us. He didn't seem to care at all about the bigger me. It seemed for a while that my days were much happier. I was suddenly a better mom. I was able to interact with my three kids in a way that I thought would make everyone proud of me. I was not just making it through the day but we were actually having fun. We read stories, played games, and sang lots of silly songs. Our house was neat and clean. I walked my son to kindergarten every single day and even had dinner prepared each evening by 5:00 pm. We had some amazing family times in the southern California sunshine. I was proud to be stay at home mom. I remember having friends and neighbors come over and comment that my house was always clean or that they would never want me to visit their homes without notice. I would just laugh. *Ha. If they only knew.*

Even still, I knew the darkness was still there, just under the surface. I could feel it. Entwined in my laugher and smiles was fear. Fear that the darkness had the power to bring me back down. *When is it coming back? When is it going to overtake me? Shake it off! Stop it! Just enjoy these moments. You are going to ruin everything.* I know

now that I had been experiencing post-partum depression. As I read through the symptoms it is overwhelmingly clear. The only symptom that I did not feel was disconnected from my baby. My kids were the only things that brought me any joy. My sadness would lift for just a moment as I watched them sleep. Holding my baby gave me hope and a purpose. I probably held on to them a little too tightly. I know now I should have sought help. I probably should have been medicated. But I made it through. Somehow, I made it through.

I knew the
darkness was
still there,
just under the
surface.

Chapter Seven

The Road of Perception

I am in the kitchen cooking dinner. I can't see her, but I know exactly where she is. *Sesame Street* has just ended so she is perched on the back of the sofa with her little feet resting gently on the window sill, her little round face and button nose pressed firmly against the glass. She's squinting her big brown eyes against the glare of the San Diego sun. Although she can't read a clock, she knows exactly what time it is. She is waiting and anticipating for her favorite part of the day. She can barely speak but I can make out the words even in her excitement, "Dada hoonnne!" Her daddy is home.

He comes bouncing and singing up the walk still dressed in his military fatigues. *How is he always so happy and carefree?* She toddles to the front door clapping and squealing as he walks in. She throws her hands up, "Pick em up Dada, pick em up!"

55

Waiting for Daddy

"Sure thing baby girl," he tells her as he reaches down and flies her up and into his arms. Once again, her day is made. Her delighted laughter is a signal to her big brother and sister who soon come thundering out of the bedroom to join in the celebration. Daddy is home! Everyone is happy ... at least they appear to be.

As they engage in a boisterous game of tickle fighting I get dinner on the table. I have made things that everyone is sure to like; fried pork chops, macaroni and cheese, green beans, and of course sweet tea. "Hey babe, how was your day?" I ask him. He is still playing with the kids but I am hoping he will look up long enough to see that I am wearing a cute summer sundress and that I have fixed my hair. I am hoping he will see and appreciate how well I am doing today. Before the kids and I moved to join him in San Diego we talked about my depression.

"No one wants to be around a bummer, Don," he told me, "you really going to have to perk up some."

Got it. Don't be a bummer. Perk up. I'm not sure if he didn't hear me, but he didn't answer and he didn't seem to notice my efforts. My heart sank. Before we sat down to eat I had to excuse myself to the bathroom. I was really hoping that no one would notice my tears. I dash in and wash my face. I look in the mirror and remind myself. *Perk up. Don't be a bummer. No one wants to be around a bummer. Okay. I'm good.* I return to the table with a smile. We have a very pleasant dinner and head out to the park afterwards. At the park we chase the kids around. They treat us to various feats on the monkey bars and swing sets. "Look Momma!" and "Watch me Daddy!" were coming from each piece of equipment as they dazzled us with their tricks. We are all laughing and having such a good time. He and I even held hands and talked as the kids ran about and played. We are such a cute young family. *What's not to be happy about? This was a good idea. Moving here was just what we needed.* I can't help but smile at this picture. *Everyone can be happy in California, even me.* As it turns out he did have a good day and as far as he knew, so did I.

⌘ ⌘ ⌘ ⌘ ⌘ ⌘ ⌘ ⌘ ⌘ ⌘ ⌘ ⌘

I made some new friends with the moms in my son's kindergarten class. I have even volunteered as one of the room moms. I would spend many of my mornings with his class. The other moms and I traded off childcare so it was easy for each of to stay involved. After school we would let all the kids play on the playground in the school yard. I could sit and visit with the other moms. Some were Navy wives but some were not. There was such a mix of cultures and people. We talked out the challenges and rewards of motherhood. One of the moms even invited us to church. Church? I hadn't considered going to church in such a long time. My mind immediately went back to the sermons from my childhood. I was just starting to feel a little better about myself. I'm not sure if I want to mess that up just yet. Apparently she could see the concern on my face. She reassured me that is was a great church. That people were very nice and friendly. Little did she know that it wasn't the people I was worried about. I can deal with people. She talked about how great the children's church was. Children's church, hmmm? That must be like Sunday school. Sunday school was good. In Sunday school you talked about how much Jesus loves you. My kids needed that. They needed to know that. Maybe I should go back to Sunday school. The message is kinder and gentler there. She was so persistent that I had no choice but to agree. *Now where is my Bible?*

So we all went to church. She was right. Everyone was so welcoming. They greeted us as we came in. They helped us get the children checked in to their proper rooms. These were the happiest people that I had ever been around. They were almost weird they were so happy. *What is wrong with these people? Is this some kind of cult?* Nonetheless, I sat down and prepared myself to hear the sermon. I was so intrigued by the message that was being shared that I was literally sitting on the edge of my seat the whole time. The pastor spoke of God's love for all of us. He talked about how we are all forgiven because Jesus had died on the cross. He talked about God's grace and mercy. *What? Where did he get this stuff? Was this the same God that I had heard about as a kid?* At one point I was sure the pastor was looking directly at me when he said, "There is nothing you can do to earn God's love. You don't have to. You already have it. God already loves you. He always has."

My husband looked at me and asked, "Are you okay?" Apparently, I was crying. Tears were streaming down my face. I hadn't even noticed. I felt as though something heavy was lifted off of me that day. A tremendous burden was gone. He was a pastor. He wasn't allowed to lie and he told me, specifically me, that God already loved me. I chose to believe him.

⌘ ⌘ ⌘ ⌘ ⌘ ⌘ ⌘ ⌘ ⌘ ⌘ ⌘ ⌘

For God so loved the world
(I am a part of the world)
that He gave His only son ...
—John 3:16

⌘ ⌘ ⌘ ⌘ ⌘ ⌘ ⌘ ⌘ ⌘ ⌘ ⌘ ⌘

I can't for the life of me remember the name of that church. I remember that the church was non-denominational, and I only remember that because before I went there, I had no idea what it meant and I had to research it ahead of time to make sure it didn't mean "cult." I barely remember the name of the friend who invited me but I remember the faces of her children and the many fun times our families had together over the next year. I will never forget how her invitation changed my heart and therefore changed my life. God loves me. *Now where is my Bible?* This time I actually took the time to find it and started to read it.

Even though my faith was being renewed, we still experienced a lot of challenges. We appeared to be a very happy young family and for the most part we were. We had so much fun together but after the kids were asleep we seemed more like just friends or roommates than a married couple. Our marriage was painfully void of intimacy. This only concerned me sometimes. I was still very uncomfortable with all the weight I had gained. I had long since ditched my sweats and oversized t-shirts but I hadn't strayed too far from the idea of "draping and covering." Before moving to California, I had convinced myself that I did not care about the extra weight. I even saw it as a punishment for my husband for the way I perceived he had treated me. But now, I had to admit that I did care. I was in California, the land of pretty and perfect people. I felt very out of place. My level of self-hate, negative body image, and low self-esteem was out of control. My husband finally said that he loved me very much but he just wasn't attracted to me like he had once been. He appreciated all that I did for him and the kids but he just didn't have the same feelings. The thrill was gone. As much as I wanted to be angry I couldn't be. I felt like I deserved it. I felt like if I didn't even like the way that I looked, how could I realistically expect someone else to. My answer was that I couldn't. So I didn't.

Now, you are probably wondering, "How big was she? What she needing to be lifted-out-the-house-with-a-crane kind of big? Was she be-the-star-of-your-own-reality-show kind of big?" No, I was neither of those. I was just bigger-than-I-was-used-to kind of big.

I was the ashamed-to-go-to-my-class-reunion-because-I-was-a-cute-dance-team-kind-of-girl kind of big. I was the these-jeans-no-longer-fit-and-you-have-to-stop-refusing-to-buy-a-bigger-size kind of big. I was just bigger than I wanted to be. There were many times later in my life that I would have gladly traded places with the size that I was then, but it didn't really matter the size. What really mattered was my perception of myself and it was off … way off! Because of it, I accepted a lot less from our relationship than I really wanted. I made myself be happy with the fact that my family was together. I found joy in my children. I took great pride in being their mother and I was content with my role as a wife. On the surface, everything looked lovely.

⌘ ⌘ ⌘ ⌘ ⌘ ⌘ ⌘ ⌘ ⌘ ⌘ ⌘ ⌘

My husband lost his mother. It was very unexpected and he took it very hard. Shortly after that he decided to request an early discharge from the Navy. As much as I thought this was a really bad idea, I decided to support him. I understood that his heart was hurting and he had the desire to be closer to his family. I had been there. I knew it was something that he felt he need to do. Still, I was concerned. We had no plan. I was concerned about what type of job he would have once he got out of the Navy. He was a sonar technician. How would that translate to a job in the real world? A world without guaranteed hours and guaranteed pay? A world without fully funded health insurance? I was concerned about where we would live. We had three young children. We had no savings. Once the Navy moved us back to Texas they would be out of our lives forever. We would be on our own. It was a safety net and a support system that I had grown very used to. As we drove back to Texas … I prayed.

⌘ ⌘ ⌘ ⌘ ⌘ ⌘ ⌘ ⌘ ⌘ ⌘ ⌘ ⌘

The Lord is my shepherd; I shall not want.
He maketh me to lie down in green pastures:
he leadeth me beside the still waters.
He restoreth my soul: he leadeth me in the
paths of righteousness for his name's sake.
Yea, though I walk through the valley of
the shadow of death, I will fear no evil:
for thou art with me; thy rod and thy staff they
comfort me. Thou preparest a table before me
in the presence of mine enemies: thou anointest
my head with oil; my cup runneth over.
Surely goodness and mercy shall follow
me all the days of my life: and I will
dwell in the house of the Lord forever.

—Psalm 23

⌘ ⌘ ⌘ ⌘ ⌘ ⌘ ⌘ ⌘ ⌘ ⌘ ⌘ ⌘

Even though I didn't completely understand this entire prayer, I knew it brought me peace. It made me feel like God was with me. So I prayed and I tried to maintain my positive attitude and support for my husband's decision. As it turned out there was good reason for my concerns.

Chapter Eight

A Fork in the Road

"**M**omma?" she whispers softly. I jumped up immediately.

"I'm right here baby." I reassure her. "What do you need?"

"I want to go home." She sobs.

"I know you do but it's not time yet." I say to her as I fight back the tears. She's been in the hospital over two weeks now and the doctors are still not quite sure what is wrong with her. Her little face is so swollen from the enlarged lymph nodes. She has dark circles under her once bright brown eyes. I crawl into bed with her and scoop her into my arms. She is still so warm. Her fever has not subsided. *What is wrong with my baby?* I cradle and rock her until she falls back to sleep. School will be starting next week and instead of her first day of kindergarten I am so afraid that she will still be right here in this bed at the children's hospital. The tears are streaming down my face now. I am so scared. I feel so alone. I decide to sing to her to make us both feel just a bit better. "Jesus loves me this I know. For the Bible tells me so. Little ones to Him belong. They are weak but He is strong."

⌘ ⌘ ⌘ ⌘ ⌘ ⌘ ⌘ ⌘ ⌘ ⌘ ⌘ ⌘

Oh dear God, I am so scared. My baby girl is so sick. Please help us. Please fix whatever is broken. Help the doctors figure out what is wrong with her so they can treat it. Please don't take her. I just don't think I can take it. Please don't take my baby.

⌘ ⌘ ⌘ ⌘ ⌘ ⌘ ⌘ ⌘ ⌘ ⌘ ⌘ ⌘

I finally fall asleep too. After what seems like just minutes, the door swings open and the team of doctors enter. We are both startled awake. "No! Get out!" My baby screams and jumps out the bed before I can comfort her. She hides under the sink in the corner and refuses to come out. She has had so many tests. She has been poked and prodded for days. I look at my little girl huddled in the dark corner under the sink. She is starring pleadingly at me. She is so afraid. I can see her shaking.

"That's enough." I tell them. "She can't take any more today. She is only 5. Please let her rest now."

The lead doctor considers arguing with me, but after seeing my determination he ushers everyone out of the room. He then turns to me and reassures me that they will figure out what is wrong. "That's fine, but not today." I coax my baby from under the sink and just sit on the floor holding her in my lap. I stroke her hair and once again rock her and sing to her. She seems so much smaller than before we got here. I'm just not sure how much more of this either one of us can take.

While we were in the hospital, my husband was working and taking care of the other kids. Since the hospital is over an hour from our home and parking was so expensive, he doesn't make it to visit very often. We have very little money. I have no money for food or for even the most basic needs like tampons. At this point I am running out of clean clothes. I am tired, scared, and hungry. I try to sound confident when I tell her that God will fix it. The next day my best friend showed up. She brought snacks, money, tampons, laughter, and hope. She brought love and comfort. She brought a stuffed bear for my baby girl. It was the first time that I had seen her smile in nearly two weeks. My friend sat with my daughter while I took a shower and washed my hair. She gave me time to go and wash my clothes. It's amazing how being clean and refreshed can change your outlook.

We took my daughter out to the playroom that was just down the hall from her room so she could watch a movie and play with dolls. I had not known this place existed until then. It was just what we needed. Although my daughter was still sick this playtime really brightened her spirits. She spent another week in the hospital, twenty-one days total. The doctors finally figured out why she was so sick.

She was diagnosed with and finally treated for Lymphoreticulosis, Cat Scratch Fever. Yes, it is really a thing.

My Baby On the Mend From Cat Scratch Fever

The fear of losing my daughter took a big toll on me. After bringing her home from the hospital I began having trouble sleeping. I was constantly checking on all three children as they slept at night. Sometimes I would just sit in the dark in their bedrooms and listen to them breathe. When I did sleep I would have horrible nightmares. In each of these dreams I would lose a child, sometimes more than one. I would frequently wake up crying or screaming. I once again found myself struggling with depression. This time was worse than it had ever been. In the past I had struggled the most when my husband was not around. He has not witnessed the full brunt of my symptoms before now. He was unsure of what to do. I could not bring myself out of it. I was sinking fast. His panic forced me to take action.

Finally, I reached out to my mom. I confessed everything that I was feeling. I told her that I felt hopeless. I was so scared. I told her that felt like I wanted to die but I was afraid of death because I wasn't sure that I would go to heaven and I was more afraid of hell than I was of living, but not by much. She immediately started making phone calls and soon I had an appointment for therapy. After the first appointment the psychiatrist and my therapist suggested that I needed inpatient treatment but I was against it. I felt that I needed to be there to take care of my children. They agreed to let me start as an outpatient, but if there was not marked improvement they would push for inpatient care. I was soon diagnosed with severe clinical depression and anxiety. I was also prescribed an antidepressant. With the weekly therapy and medication, I was able to think clearly. My mind was no longer racing. I was no longer paralyzed by fear and for the first time in years, I felt like I was going to be alright.

I was diagnosed with severe clinical depression and anxiety.

I did not have the same confidence in the relationship with my husband. Our marriage had always been fragile. The years after leaving the military had not been easy. My husband had changed jobs many times leaving me feeling very insecure about our future. This insecurity led to frequent arguments about money. We fought about the lack of it and how it was spent. My husband's philosophy on spending was that it was just money and we could always make more. I felt that we did not have much of it and we needed to be very careful about how we spent it. Money wasn't the only thing that caused conflict. We could not agree on the shared responsibility of raising the children, household chores, what movie to watch, or just about anything else. We separated and reconciled at least three more times. Each time it had been his decision to leave. We had been married for over twelve years, but had spent over half of the time apart. Although I had attempted to file for divorce once before, I had not been able to follow through with it. This time, after lengthy separation I was ready. After 12 years, I had seriously had enough. There was no arguing at this point. There was no drama. We met at the courthouse. We signed the papers and then we went to lunch, together. We apologized to each other and went our separate ways.

I thought the hardest part would be telling my children. It took me two days to prepare what I was going to say to them. I was ready to comfort and reassure them. They were 11, 10, and 7 at the time. I sat them down and told them that their father and I were now divorced. I explained that we were no longer married and that there was no chance of us working things out. I explained that we both still loved them very much and that we were both still their parents. My son seemed surprised. "Really?" he asked, "I thought y'all were already divorced. I had no idea that you were still married."

My oldest daughter seemed relieved, "Oh good. I was thinking that it wasn't going to work out with dad. I just didn't know how to tell you. I'm glad you know." Then she gave me a big hug and a kiss, as if it was her responsibility to reassure me.

My youngest daughter had the most unexpected reaction, "Does this mean that we can have Christmas at two different places? Cause that would be kind of cool."

Now, I would not be so naïve to say or think that the divorce did not affect them. Divorce is devastating to everyone involved. I am just saying that by the time we made it official my kids had already moved on from the idea of us being a family. Although I felt it was what I needed to do at the time, I was not as advanced in my thinking as they were. I was still mourning the loss of my family. I was disillusioned that I had not been able to make it work. I was not able to keep my family unit together. The possibility of my fairy tale life had officially died. As a wife, I had failed.

The possibility
of my fairy
tale life had
officially died.

Chapter Nine

Traveling Alone

"May I speak with Donya?" asked a voice on the phone.

"Yes? This is Donya?" I reply.

"I'm calling from the police department," the voice continued, "We have your son pulled over in your car."

I shook my head in disbelief, "That is not possible. My son is downstairs in the parking lot getting his shoes out the car and my son in only thirteen. He does not drive. This must be some kind of mistake."

We live in a very small town. Everybody knows everybody here. The voice on the phone assures me that it is my son. She knows me. She knows my son. She and I had gone to high school together. The officer who had my son pulled over had graduated with us as well.

My 13-Year-Old Auto "Borrower"

Our boys all play baseball together. There is not mistake. "We don't want to press any charges. We just need you to come and get him and your car."

That would be great, I think to myself, *but I HAVE NO CAR!* Luckily, I was able to get a friend to take me the few miles away to pick up my car and my child. When I get there my son is sitting in the back of the police car with tears running down his face. He looks terrified. I am furious. *What is wrong with this kid? Has he seriously lost his mind. Exactly how wrong is it to strangle your kid in front of the police?* The officer gets out of the car first. I'm not sure if it is because he sees the look on my face or if it is because he is also the parent of a teenaged son but he rushes to me and says, "Now Donya, I know you are angry but it won't make things any better if you kill the boy.

He's pretty scared. I don't think he'll be doing anything like this again."

I just stare blankly at the officer. I do not even know what to say.

"If it makes you feel any better," he continues, "he was real cool until he found out we had called his mom. When he heard you were on your way it put the fear of God in him!"

Although I understood what he was trying to say, it did not make me feel any better. I felt that if he was so afraid of me he never would have taken my car in the first place. Finally, after lecturing him on not breaking the law and being a good citizen, the officer releases the boy to my custody. I look at him and ask, "What exactly is your problem? What the heck makes you think you can take my car? What makes you think that you can just joyride around town and I won't find out about it?"

His response still astounds me "Well," he shrugged, "I've done it before and you didn't know."

Well I know now, don't I?

⌘ ⌘ ⌘ ⌘ ⌘ ⌘ ⌘ ⌘ ⌘ ⌘ ⌘ ⌘

Two of my children are now in middle school and one is in elementary school. I am a full time mom, I am a full time student, and I work full time. I am also single, raising my kids without much help from their father. I am trying hard to make it all work. My son being pulled over by the police opened my eyes to the fact that I may be out of touch with the potential trouble that was out there for my kids to find. I still viewed them all as babies. They were growing up quickly and they needed a better foundation.

We had been going to church over the years, but in the past year or so our attendance had dropped. It was important to me to instill the right values in our family. I wanted them to come to know Jesus. I wanted them to learn to trust what the Bible said. The children had visited a church with their friends that seemed to have a strong youth program so we started going as a family. It was a non-denominational, family-centered church. It seemed to be just what we needed. The church presented the Bible in a practical way that helped me understand how to implement God's Word in my daily life.

The goal of the youth program was to help preteens and teens make God-based decisions in their lives. It gave my older two kids accountability with the new friends they were making. My youngest daughter participated in the children's program. She was starting to understand that Jesus loved her, not just because I told her but because it was true. We were at church every Wednesday and every Sunday. For several years all the kids participated in summer church camps. I would have to work very hard to save or raise all of the money necessary, but I made sure it happened. I felt like I was doing everything I could to give my children a strong foundation.

I was growing stronger in my faith as well. I had let go of the misconceptions I had learned as I child. I had let go of the notion that God was an ever present score keeper holding every wrong against us. I was learning more of God's love for us. I was starting to understand the grace and mercy He has for us as His children. Each time there was a call for salvation I wanted to run to the front and except Jesus into my heart all over again. I didn't actually do it, but I was so excited about the opportunity to know for sure that I would have eternal life in heaven that I wanted to. I could feel my hope being restored. I was happier than I had ever been. I was starting to feel like my life had purpose. I still had a lot to learn but I was getting there.

The words in the Bible were starting to make more sense to me. They were not just stories of things that happened long ago. I was starting to see them as more of a road map of how to make decisions each day. I was starting to love my Bible instead of fear it. I felt like I talked openly with my kids about making the right decisions. I warned against the perils of drug use. I tried to keep the doors of communication open for them to come to me with any problems or concerns that they may be having. I told them that although I may be disappointed if they made mistakes I would always love them. I would always be there to help them make the right decisions. I thought I had done everything that I could to set them up for success. I was wrong.

⌘ ⌘ ⌘ ⌘ ⌘ ⌘ ⌘ ⌘ ⌘ ⌘ ⌘ ⌘

After a couple of years, the older two kids started to drift away from their church friends. They started to get into a lot of trouble in school. The calls from the vice principals were frequent:

"Mrs. White, I have your son in my office. He had been disrupting class and will not settle down."

"Mrs. White, we're going to need you to come and get your daughter. She just told the teacher to get out of her face."

"Umm, Mrs. White, your daughter has just been in another fight."

"Mrs. White, your son has been absent for several days. Has he been sick?"

The number and the reasons for the calls go on and on. Each time I would try to find the appropriate consequence for the behavior I was being called about. Each time I would try to talk to them about why it was important to maintain the appropriate standard of conduct at school. Many times I would lose my temper. I would scream and yell and cry. I felt like a terrible mother. *What is wrong with them? Why are they behaving this way? They know this type of behavior is not acceptable. We are not these people. We don't fight and skip school. We are respectable people. They are good kids. They went to church camp. They love Jesus! Why are they doing this to me?*

I started to take each infraction personally. I had become so angry with both of them. I would frequently ground them to the house for unreasonable periods of time so that I did not have to be concerned about what they may be doing while they were away. Nothing seemed to make a difference. Their bad behavior continued. For several years I attempted to keep them out of trouble, but nothing seemed to work. When I was faced with the possibility that they were experimenting with drugs I had to do something different, something drastic.

Since they would not listen to me, I thought perhaps they would listen to their father. The summer before they were a sophomore and junior in high school, I sent them to live with him. I tried to tell myself that it was for their own good. To some extent it was for me too. I was tired and frustrated. I wanted a break. Besides, their father would be more stern. He would be able to make them do what they were supposed to do. I must admit the thought of him having to experience the everyday ins and outs of parenting teens made the idea even more appealing. I never felt that this would be a permanent arrangement, I just thought it was the best thing for a little while. Again, I was wrong.

Their bad choices continued. They were skipping school just as they had before. The fights continued. The disregard for and disrespect towards their teachers continued. They found and started hanging out with the same type of kids they had been getting in trouble with before. My ex-husband was frustrated and overwhelmed just as I had been. The situation in their household became volatile. Their frequent arguments and outburst led to the police being called multiple times. They had been living with their father for just a few months when I received a frantic phone call from my son. He was screaming and yelling for me to come and pick me up immediately. I could hear his father screaming and yelling in the background, "Come and get him! Right now! I'm not putting up with this anymore!"

I was not sure what the conflict was, but I knew that I could not allow this to continue. At that moment I realized that it was unreasonable to for me to expect their father, who had very little parenting experience to this point, to know how to effectively handle out of control teenagers. It was not fair to anyone involved. I had been parenting them their entire lives and I couldn't figure it out. No matter what was going on with them I would have to find out a way to fix it. I went that same day and picked up my son. At the end of the school semester I went and brought my daughter home as well. They were my babies and my responsibility.

Chapter Ten

A Slight Detour

"**D**onya, he needs you to sign this invoice," she says as she peeks into my office. I look up from my desk and the clerk is smiling awkwardly at me. She looks suspiciously amused.

"Okay," I finally respond, "I'll be right there, but you are perfectly capable of signing an invoice." As I exit my office I notice it's the new salesman for our waffle vendor. He is such a nice man. He had only been our salesman for a couple of months, but I think I have talked to him more than all the other vendors in the 3 years that I have been managing this hotel.

"Hello," he smiles. "Sorry to bother you. I just need your signature."

"Oh, it's no problem, but you don't ever have to wait on me. Each of the clerks is authorized to sign for the delivery."

"I don't mind waiting," he assures me.

Why do I have this stupid smile on my face? Did I just giggle? What is wrong with me? I try to act normal and thank him for being so efficient and having such great customer service. *Now he's the one with the stupid smile. What is this, high school?*

"Well if you need anything else, you just give me a call," he says. "Do you have my cell phone number?"

"No," I answer, trying to play it cool, "but if we need something we usually just call your office. I wouldn't want to bother you on your cell phone."

"It's no bother. Here's my number," he says and hands me his business card.

"Thank you so much," I take the card and know I am smiling a little too big, "but I promise I won't call you unless it's an emergency."

"Well," he says with a smirk, "I'm single so you can call whenever you want."

"Haha!" I laugh, "Well I'm single too so I guess that works out pretty well." We both laugh at our silly joke and part ways. As he walks out the door the desk clerk is beaming.

"He likes you!" she gloats. "That man was flirting with you!" she practically screams.

"No he wasn't," I roll my eyes at her, "you think everyone is flirting. He was just being nice. That man has absolutely no interest in me." I am done with this conversation and head back into my office. No sooner than I had sat down she pops her head back into the door.

"Boss lady, you have a call on line one," I hear her smugness.

Why is she being so goofy? I might have to have her drug tested. "This is Donya, how can I help you?"

"Hi Donya, this is Randy. I'm your waffle guy," he starts to explain. I laugh out loud.

"Yes, Randy I know who you are. You were just standing at my counter."

"Oh yeah, I was."

Why does he sound so nervous? Is he regretting giving his cell number to a customer? I bet he wants the number back.

"Um," he continues, "Were you serious when you said you were single?"

"Yes," I replied, "I wouldn't joke about that because I don't think it's very funny." I laughed to let him know I <u>was</u> joking about that. He laughed too.

"Well, I was wondering if maybe you would like to go out to dinner, with me?"

Really? Did he just ask me out, like on a date? This sort of thing never happens to me. Do people even still go out on dates?

"Yes, Randy. I would love to go out to dinner with you." I had to answer quickly before I thought about it and changed my mind.

"Really? I was sure you would say no. I thought you would be really nice about it and let me down easy but that you would say no."

"Well you're stuck now," I laughed, "because I said yes." We both laughed again. I gave him my number so that we could talk later and make arrangements for our date. As I hang up the phone, I see the desk clerk standing in my door way looking victorious.

"I told you," she said, "I told you that man was flirting with you. He looks for you every time he comes in. He likes you."

"Okay," I concede, "Maybe you are right. Maybe he was flirting a little."

⌘ ⌘ ⌘ ⌘ ⌘ ⌘ ⌘ ⌘ ⌘ ⌘ ⌘ ⌘

I had recently ended a nearly 3-year relationship. I was tired of dating and tired of the complications that came along with it. I was done. My kids and I would be just fine alone. We had made it this far and we would carry on. *God if you have a man for me you are going to have to just drop him on my door step with a note from you. I apparently am no good at making my own choices.* One thing that being married had taught me was how to recognize what I did not want in a relationship. I did not want to be more unhappy than happy. I expected relationships to be work but I would no longer accept that all of the work would come from me.

My kids did not share my willingness to remain single. They felt that I needed to be married. Since I had divorced their father, they had been on the lookout for a new husband for me. They were constantly pointing out their teachers, coaches, and youth group leaders. They would even want to fix me up with the single fathers of their friends. Their attempts were nothing short of comical. I wasn't even safe in the grocery store. My oldest daughter would scan the contents of men's grocery carts to determine if they may be single. Then she would try to guide me in his direction so that we could accidentally meet. My youngest daughter would mostly find me men on TV. She had a very high opinion of my dating capability. They were happy to hear about my pending date.

Although we were both excited about the idea of going out together, it took us several attempts to make that first date happen. On the first try, I came down with strep throat. The next time, he had to cancel because his house had been broken into. Later, we had to postpone because of Hurricane Katrina and again because of Hurricane Rita. *God are You trying to tell me something? Is this you trying to stop this date from happening? You know I don't do well with hints. Please scream at me or push me down or something to let me know if I am not supposed to do this.*

I didn't hear anything that sounded like God, so I decided to not worry much about it. I didn't feel at the time that it would end up being a romantic relationship. He didn't seem to be my type and I wasn't sure that we had much in common. However, he was very nice and at the very least I felt that we could be friends. Because of the many delays we were able to talk on the phone a lot. I discovered that he too, was a single parent. He had a daughter in college and a high school-aged son who lived with him. He had been transferred to our area from Phoenix, Arizona but wasn't expecting to be here very long because he was supposed to transfer to Colorado next. He was just a little older than me and seemed to be very confident in who he was as a person. I loved the fact that we did not have to pretend to be people that we were not. We joked that we were just too old to play dating games.

Finally, just over a month after agreeing to go out, we had our first date. I remember him asking me about my hobbies. I explained that with three children in various sports and activities I didn't really have time for hobbies but my favorite thing to do was to watch major league baseball games either in person or on TV. He looked astonished. *Oh no, he doesn't like baseball. Now we can't even be friends.*

"Who told you to say that?" he questioned.

Really? You are new in town? Who do I know that you know, silly man?

He explained that baseball was his favorite sport. He had played his whole life—even played professionally in the minor leagues for a short while. I was in first date heaven! We spent the whole rest of the evening talking about baseball and our favorite teams. He was so knowledgeable. I was very impressed. He was funny and charming. I smiled a lot that night.

When I got home, my kids were waiting for me. I told them that I actually like him a lot but I was afraid that he may be a bit too normal for us. Our life had always been a bit chaotic and I wasn't sure just anyone could handle being a part of it. Before he even got home that night he called me.

"I'm sure this is against some dating rule but would you like to go out again some time, like next weekend?"

"Well aren't you just a rebel," I laughed, "You are just throwing caution to the wind. I would love to. I'll talk to you tomorrow."

God is that You? Was that a note? If this is not of You then please put a stop to it. The second date went as scheduled. No hurricanes, major illness, and criminal activity got in the way to postpone it. By the end of the second date I was pretty sure that I was falling in love. *Uh oh. God, I'm really going to need your help here.*

The Start of Something Special

Chapter Eleven

Moving Right Along

"**M**om! She won't be still!" my youngest daughter yells to me as she tries to comb her 4-year-old cousin's hair.

"Aunt Donya, I can't find my other shoe," whines the 9-year-old.

"Please, stop whining!" I yell down the hall, " ... and somebody help her find her shoe!" My oldest daughter is supposed to be in charge of helping her get ready but she is in the bathroom putting on makeup. The boys appear from out of their room.

"We're ready." They proclaim. I take one look at them and realize that they are not ready.

"No you are not, neither of you. Go wash your face, brush your teeth, and then brush your hair." I tell them as I rush into the kitchen

Trying to Make it On Our Own

to make lunches. "Make sure he does everything I just said." I yell back to my son. "He is only 5. He is going to need some help." I have put each older child in charge of a younger cousin. Between all of us we can make this work. "Deodorant! Don't forget deodorant!" These instructions go out to all. As we are headed out the door we grab backpacks and lunch bags. As I sign last minute permission slips and homework corrections I distribute kisses to the oldest two who are headed to the bus stop and usher the four smaller ones into the car.

Oh no, I forgot to brush my own teeth! I rush back into the house. As I am standing in front of my bathroom sink quickly brushing my teeth I take a moment to look at myself in the mirror. *What are you thinking? What makes you think you can handle three more kids?*

Your own kids are nearly self-sufficient why would you take on these babies? They need you, that's why. Back out the door I go with a bagel between my teeth and coffee cup in my hand. "Who's ready for a great day?" I ask as I slide into the car.

"We are!" scream the little ones. I laugh along with their enthusiasm as I pull out of the drive way. My 12-year-old daughter just sighs and rolls her eyes. She thinks I'm crazy. She might be right.

Just a few weeks before I had been talking to my cousin. We had always had a very close relationship. We had grown up together and were more like sisters. In fact, my mother had taken her in when she was about the age of her oldest daughter. She had recently lost her home and was trying to find another one. She was also juggling raising her children and going to nursing school. She was staying in a hotel and trying to drive her children back and forth to school. She was driving over 40 miles roundtrip each day. Sometimes she was not able to get to them as they were dropped off by the school bus in their old neighborhood and they would have to wait for her to get there. Since they no longer lived in the house in that neighborhood, the kids had no place to go while they waited. It was clear that she needed help. I offered to have her children stay with me so that she could find another place for them to live and focus on school until the semester was over. Although I knew it would be difficult, it seemed to be the best situation for everyone.

I offered to have her children stay with me.

Only months before my son and oldest daughter had returned from an attempt to live with their father. Since their return, their behavior seemed to have calmed down quite a bit. There were no calls from the high school for discipline or attendance issues and their grades were improving. Even their choice of friends had improved. My youngest daughter was struggling with the added family members. She had enjoyed the time that her brother and sister were gone. She enjoyed the illusion of being an only child. She had been very happy to have me all to herself. Now not only were her brother and sister back home, but there were now three extra children she had to share my attention with. She was not amused. As hard as I tried it was difficult to make sure each child got all of the attention that they needed. I passed out lots of hugs, kisses, and encouraging words but there were six of them and one of me. Even still, as a group they felt loved and protected. At least I hope they did.

⌘ ⌘ ⌘ ⌘ ⌘ ⌘ ⌘ ⌘ ⌘ ⌘ ⌘ ⌘

My new relationship was also going well, but I was concerned about how my increased family size would affect us. When I explained to Randy that I was going to be taking care of three more children he just hugged me, kissed my forehead, and told me I was an incredible woman. My main reason for telling him was to give him the option to end the relationship. We had not been dating very long. It wasn't reasonable to expect him to be a part of this change. I wasn't sure how it would affect my free time and there was no reason for my decision to affect his life. He didn't leave. He didn't complain. He still came to visit and even offered to help when he could. I was absolutely amazed by his kind heart.

As we continued to date we found that we had so many things in common. Some of the parallel events in our lives where almost creepy. We had both been married before and both divorced. The date of both of our fist marriages was July 25. His previous mother-in-law's name was Beverly. My mother's name is Beverly. My previous mother-in-law's name was Joyce. That was his mother's name. We had to laugh at the similarities. We decided that maybe God was giving us a "do over." If that was the case, we determined that we should try and not mess it up.

⌘ ⌘ ⌘ ⌘ ⌘ ⌘ ⌘ ⌘ ⌘ ⌘ ⌘ ⌘

Just before the little children had moved in I had purchased a new home. I was so proud of this achievement because I had done it all by myself. I had worked hard and saved all my bonuses and income tax returns for several years. I had been referred to a special finance company that specialized in helping "people like me." They convinced me that because I was a single parent with one income it would be difficult for me to find and afford a home using traditional financing. They assured me that their plan was the perfect option. They claimed to be Christians connected to a large reputable church in our area. They showed me their website with all the testimonies of satisfied clients. I trusted them. I was wrong.

Less than a year after moving into the house I received a call from the builder. They had just realized that the finance company that I was using had never actually paid them for my house. The purchase had never been funded. It appears that they had been swindled as well. I had given my entire savings of just over $12,000 to this company. I had been paying them a mortgage payment of $1,200 per month for almost a year. They had taken the money and disappeared. The phone numbers that I had previously called were disconnected. Even the website was gone. It seemed like a lot to do for the money that they had taken from me. It was everything that

I had, but to me it didn't seem like enough money for them to go through so much effort. Then I found out that that it wasn't just me. They had five deals with this builder alone. The authorities suspected there were others but were still investigating. The only option I had was to find a legitimate finance company. Although I found that unlike what I had been told, I easily qualified for a traditional home loan, I no longer had the ability to make a large down payment. I was going to lose my house. I was devastated. That night I after all the kids where in bed I cried out to God.

⌘ ⌘ ⌘ ⌘ ⌘ ⌘ ⌘ ⌘ ⌘ ⌘ ⌘ ⌘

I need you. I have no idea what I am going to do. I have all these kids here who are depending on me. Please show me what to do. Please help me.

⌘ ⌘ ⌘ ⌘ ⌘ ⌘ ⌘ ⌘ ⌘ ⌘ ⌘ ⌘

How did this happen? How where they able to just come and take everything that I had? How could I be this stupid?

I called Randy and I cried. "Everything is going to be okay," he said. "Do you have all the information for the men you have been dealing with?" he asked. He was so angry that someone had taken advantage of me. He was even more angry that they had made me cry.

"I am going to track them down," he insisted. "One way or another I am going to get your money back!"

I started to laugh. I know he was completely serious and my situation was desperate, but this show of chivalry made me laugh. The next day I found a rental house close by so that all the kids could remain in their current schools. Randy came over and helped us move. We packed up all my belongings and all my kids and moved us to a new house. Whenever I started to cry, he would just hold me and reassure me that everything would be alright. I had never had that in a relationship. I was usually the one holding everything together. It was a welcome change.

⌘ ⌘ ⌘ ⌘ ⌘ ⌘ ⌘ ⌘ ⌘ ⌘ ⌘ ⌘

Okay, God, I got your note. Thank You.

⌘ ⌘ ⌘ ⌘ ⌘ ⌘ ⌘ ⌘ ⌘ ⌘ ⌘ ⌘

Chapter Twelve

A Bump in the Road

"Mom, come look at your daughter," my son says as he steps into my room. "She has completely lost her mind." I can hear a lot of commotion in the hallway, but I am in my bathroom getting dressed for work. I am not sure what is going on.

"I'll be there in a minute," I yell behind him as he heads for the kitchen, "We need to leave in 10 minutes or everyone will be late!"

This should be so much easier since the little kids had returned to their mother. Each of my children only had to dress themselves now. I step into the hallway and can hardly believe my eyes. My 16-year-old daughter is flailing around in the middle of the floor. She is crying and wailing ... and literally throwing a temper tantrum that any 2-year-old would be proud of. I yell her name to get her attention.

95

"What is wrong with you? This is ridiculous! Stop it right now and get up from there. We need to leave in less than 10 minutes! Where are your clothes?" I am yelling one phrase after another. I have been pulled into this circus against my will.

At this point all she will say through a barrage of tears is, "I can't find my pants." She is wailing at the top of her lungs, "I can't find my pants!"

I ask her a number questions pertaining to the pants but all she will say is, "I can't find my pants!"

That is it. I am done. I tell her siblings to just leave her there. We have to go. I can't stay here and participate in this craziness. I tell her to go and get back in the bed. I will just have to deal with this later. It would be another couple of months before we fully understood what the problem was.

Just before (and well after) the incident with the missing pants, my daughter had been very sick. She was having multiple problem with her stomach. She had not been able to keep anything down for days. She had dark circles under her eyes and was starting to lose weight. She was a tiny girl to begin with, so weight loss for her was not good. After realizing that she was dealing with much more that a stomach virus I decided to take her to the doctor. After multiple visits, test, and even an abdominal ultrasound they were still unsure what the cause of her illness could be. The doctor decided that she was suffering from severe acid reflux. He prescribed some medicine and sent her home. She threw up twice on the way home. I assumed that the medicine they had prescribed was working because as the weeks passed she started to feel better. Her symptoms seemed to be going away, but I still felt that something was wrong.

I tried to talk to her about it, but the more I pushed the more she withdrew. I was happy that she had gained back some of the weight she lost. If I mentioned it she became very emotional. That didn't concern me too much because most teenaged girls were sensitive about their weight. Still, something was not right. She became less social. The way she dressed started to change. She just didn't seem like herself. Late one night the reason became painfully clear. I saw her standing quietly in my door way. I didn't say anything for a moment and realized she thought I was asleep. I watched as she tiptoed into my room to the far side of my bed. I assumed that she was going to crawl into bed with me as she had done on many occasions in the past. The thought made me smile since she had been so distantly lately. She was actually coming in the get something off of the floor in my room. As she stood up to leave the light from the window above my bed shone directly on her perfectly round baby bump. She was very clearly pregnant.

I sat up and flipped on the light. She froze in her tracks. In a moment she was in a crumpled, sobbing heap on my bed. She laid her head in my lap and cried for hours. She said she had broken up with her boyfriend and that he wanted nothing to do with her or the baby. He had wanted her to have an abortion because he felt like this would ruin his life. My heart broke for her. Not only was her life about to change forever in ways that she never imagined, she had been crying, going through all of this all alone for months. Although I was completely disappointed in the choices she made, I assured her that she would be just fine. I let her know that she was not alone and that we would get through this together. All of a sudden the horrible sickness, mood swings, and even the incident with the missing pants made a lot more sense.

⌘ ⌘ ⌘ ⌘ ⌘ ⌘ ⌘ ⌘ ⌘ ⌘ ⌘ ⌘

Oh God! What are we going to do? I need you now more than ever. I can't believe this has happened. What kind of mother am I? I should have been more aware of where she was and what she was doing. Maybe I was working too many hours. Maybe I was too focused on my own happiness to notice what she was doing. We talked about this. Why didn't she come to me? Please help me to do what is best for everyone. Please.

⌘ ⌘ ⌘ ⌘ ⌘ ⌘ ⌘ ⌘ ⌘ ⌘ ⌘ ⌘

The next day I called and made a doctor's appointment for her. After her first visit, we found out that she was already nearly six months pregnant. We had very little time to prepare. As I started shopping for baby supplies, the clerks at the stores would frequently as me if I was the one having the baby. Then it dawned on me, not only was my daughter becoming a mother, I would be becoming a grandmother. *What! Are you kidding me? I need some oxygen. I need to sit down. This can't really be happening.* It was happening. At 38 years old I was about to be someone's grandmother. *We are going to have to find a new name. Grandmother just does not fit me. I am way too young to be grandmother!*

Once again, I called Randy. Once again, my life was changing in an unexpected way. I completely expected this to be the time he decided to back out. Between us we already had four teenagers. If we decided to continue our relationship and get married that alone would be a lot to deal with. Adding a baby could definitely be a deal breaker. Once again, he was totally supportive and elected to stay around. After we found out that she would be having a baby boy, he showed up with the baby's first baseball gear. He said it was important that we start to little guy off with the right values. We had to be sure that he would love baseball. Again, he was able to make me laugh in what could have been a very difficult situation. He had been given several opportunities to end our relationship and each time he chose to stay. Each time I was completely surprised and touched. He didn't seem to feel like it was any big deal. He said he loved me. He insisted that he wasn't just going to leave because life got a little messy. *Well, that's new. I thought that was when and why people leave, when life gets messy. Alright God, enough notes already. I'll relax a little.*

Since my daughter was still in high school, I was concerned about how she would handle being at school each day. I knew it was not like it had been in the past. I knew that most girls where not shuttled off to some distant relative's house and forgotten about until after their baby was born. Although the stigma had lessened and teenage pregnancies seemed more common that they used to be, I was still protective of my daughter's feelings. I was pleasantly surprised to find out the number of resources that were available for pregnant teenagers in

> *I am not going to leave just because life gets a little messy.*

our school district. There was a program set up that allowed the girls to continue school. They could either remain in their regular classes or attend classes separately with other moms-to-be. Transportation to get them to and from school was also provided, and in addition to their regular coursework, they had classes on nutrition, newborn care, and parenting. They were given every opportunity to succeed and graduate.

⌘ ⌘ ⌘ ⌘ ⌘ ⌘ ⌘ ⌘ ⌘ ⌘ ⌘ ⌘

A few months later my daughter delivered a perfect and healthy baby boy. My mother, my sister, and I were in the delivery room with her. Randy, her father, her step-mother, and her siblings were all in the waiting room. As she began her journey into motherhood, her village was present and ready to help.

After she returned home from the hospital the Teen Parenting Program at her school sent a tutor. The tutor came twice a week during her six-week maternity leave. When she returned to school she was right where she should have been academically. Actually, with the individualized instruction, her grades where better than they had ever been. The school bus returned to take her to school but now it was equipped with baby seats and would take the baby to school with her as well. The program was also equipped with a fully functioning daycare. The moms had time to bond with their babies and complete their school work. Even with her unexpected blessing, with the help of this amazing program, my daughter was able to graduate high school on time with most of her village in attendance.

My Girl and Her Boy

Chapter Thirteen

Merging

"Meme! Meme!" his little voice cries out. I don't recall his mother speaking so clearly so young. He is less than a year old and I can understand most of what he says.

"Yes, my darling," I answer as I swoop him up into my arms. The love I have for this little guy is immeasurable. I had heard people talk many times about the love of grandchildren. They would explain how it is so different from anything they had ever known. I thought it would be much longer before I found out for myself but now that I had experienced the new level of love, I would not trade it for anything in the world.

"Eat?" he asked with a big smile.

"Of course my punkin, you can have whatever you want." After planting kisses all over his little face I take him into the kitchen to grant his every wish. "Strawberries? Yes. Cantaloupe? No problem. Blueberries? Why, certainly."

"Mom!" his mother protests, "You are spoiling him!"

"Okay," I reply, "I'm good with that. I'm a Meme, it's my job!" She laughs and shakes her head.

All a sudden my precious grandson is struggling to get out of my arms. He's very excited. He saying something that I can't quite understand. "Hunna hone! Hunna hone!" I look at his mother searching for translation.

She laughs again, "He's saying that Honey is home. That's what you always say when Randy walks in. Did you know that's what he calls Randy? He calls him Honey, just like you do."

Honey and the Grandboy

From that day on Randy has been known as Honey. He is my honey for sure. We are now Meme and Honey. These are titles that we are so happy to have.

Just after our grandson was born I found out that the house I was renting would no longer be available. The owner had decided to sell it to pay college tuition for his daughters. I couldn't argue with that, although I wanted to. At the same time Randy's lease was about to end on his house. We had been dating for over a year, and after a serious discussion about where our relationship was headed we decided to move our families in together. It was not a decision I was completely comfortable with but I talked myself into it by telling myself that I was just being old fashioned. *Oh stop it, Donya, I told myself, nobody goes by those rules anymore. It's not like you don't love each other. It's not like you don't know that you are going to get married. It just doesn't make any sense for you both to continue to pay rent. You could get a much better house if you combine both incomes. So just stop it before you run him off!*

We found a beautiful house with plenty of room for everyone and combined our households. Together we had four teenagers, a baby, and a dog. He also had three cats, but due to severe allergies and my extreme dislike for cats in general, they were not allowed to come. Don't get offended. After all, a cat scratch nearly killed my baby girl!

I was excited about the fact that my three kids would have a father in their lives every day. My son would have a man around to set a good example. My daughters would be able to see an example of how they should expect to be treated as wives and mothers. Randy was excited as well. He wanted his son to have a mother in his life every day. We really did feel like everyone would benefit from this arrangement.

At first everything seemed to be going well. The kids were actually friends. That did not last long. We were completely unprepared for the challenges we would face. I had this picture of *The Brady Bunch* in my head. In my version of events, we would all blend naturally. Randy and I would present a united front and make all parenting decisions together. We would discuss the best course of action and act accordingly. Any conflict would be resolved with productive and civil family meetings. We would have a total *kumbaya* existence. I was even excited about having a dog. Sadly, I discussed none of these expectations with Randy ahead of time and there was nothing in our household that happened remotely like anything I had in my head.

Randy and I had become very good single parents. Unfortunately, we remained two single parents living in the same household. We both took charge of our separate families and did not really allow the other to participate in the parenting, so we argued frequently about how to parent or things that our kids had done. Our parenting styles were completely different. I had a lot of rules. All my rules had been neatly printed on laminated sheets in the kitchen of our house. Randy didn't have many rules. He and his son where more like roommates. I don't think any method was more right than the other, just different. I am not sure it was always intentional but the kids did a pretty good job of playing their parent against the other parent. My kids constantly complained that they had to do so many

> *We remained two single parents living in the same household.*

things that their soon-to-be step brother didn't have to do. Randy's son complained that he was outnumbered. There were three them and just one of him. There was constant discontent. I can't tell you exactly the best way to combine two families, but I can certainly give you some pretty good pointers on what <u>not</u> to do.

It was not all bad. Even with the conflict there was still a lot of love in our household and the presence of our grandson was certainly a uniting factor. Everyone loved him. We would all do whatever was necessary to take care of him. He brought joy to us all.

As much as I had tried to defend him, the actions of my son were getting out of control. After receiving two late night calls from an attorney telling me he had been arrested I realized that his behavior was getting reckless. I had to think about the wellbeing of everyone else in the household. I made the decision to tell him he had to leave. Kicking a child out of your house is, in my opinion, one of the most difficult decisions a parent can ever make. Although he was 18 years old, I was terrified thinking of him in the world all alone. In my mind I was sending a 10-year-old into the lion's den. *Where will he go? What will he eat? What if he ends up homeless living under a bridge?* ... then I would waver, *but what if he brings drugs to my house? What if the police show up? There is a baby and young girls here. He is not a baby. He had several chances to do better.* I felt horribly guilty but at the same time I knew I couldn't allow his behavior to continue.

I did it. I asked him to live, then after he left I was so sad. Then I became angry. I turned my anger towards Randy. If I hadn't moved in with him, I rationalized, I would not have had to make a decision like that. I should have thanked him. It was the first of many tough decisions I would have to make regarding my children and their behavior. I have to admit that things in the household seemed to calm down a bit after that.

Even with the family conflict still present, Randy and I were sure that we loved each other and opted to move forward with our plan to get married. This time before I committed my life to marriage I prayed.

⌘ ⌘ ⌘ ⌘ ⌘ ⌘ ⌘ ⌘ ⌘ ⌘ ⌘ ⌘

God, I really feel like this is the man you sent to me. I know we are making a lot of mistakes. I know we should not have moved in together before we were married. Please forgive me for making a decision that I knew was wrong. If I am not to marry this man, please show me. I don't want to get married again when it is not Your will.

⌘ ⌘ ⌘ ⌘ ⌘ ⌘ ⌘ ⌘ ⌘ ⌘ ⌘ ⌘

I waited. I watched for signs. I waited for a house to fall on my head but nothing happened. I felt sure that this was a union that God had sanctioned—so we got married. All of our kids were there. My son walked me down the aisle. Randy's daughter served as our best man ... well, best woman. It was a beautiful day. We were all so happy. We knew we didn't have all the answers but together we were willing to find them.

Chapter Fourteen

Road Blocks and Dead Ends

"Donya?" asks the voice on the phone.

"Yes, this is Donya," I reply.

"This is the customer service department," says the voice on the phone.

"Hi. How can I help you?" I ask.

"Well, we have a guest complaint for your hotel," she sounds a little hesitant but continues, "There is a man staying at your hotel and ... ummm ... he is <u>very</u> upset because he doesn't like the pillows."

What? My mind tries to reconcile what I just heard, *What did she just say? Did she seriously just say that he didn't like his pillows? Is he aware that we are in the middle of a major hurricane? Is he aware that there are people who are actually displaced from their homes? Has this man lost his ever loving mind?*

"I'm sorry," I say, measuring the tone of my voice, "Did you just say he doesn't like his pillows?" *I must be hearing her wrong.*

"Yes, ma'am. I'm sorry to bother you with this but we are required to call the manager of the hotel if the guest insists that they want to talk with someone." I could feel the genuineness of her tone.

I knew it wasn't her fault and I was determined not to make her pay for something that was not her fault. I collect the information so I can go and speak with the guest who is upset about pillows as many of the trees on property were being uprooted and blown away by the hurricane force winds. Needless to say, I may not have been nearly as understanding as he would have liked. The stress of situations like this were starting to get to me.

One night I woke up feeling sick. As I tried to make my way to the bathroom I wasn't sure if I was going to throw up or pass out. Unfortunately, I did both. I lay on the cold tile of the bathroom floor and I cried. I cried and I prayed.

⌘ ⌘ ⌘ ⌘ ⌘ ⌘ ⌘ ⌘ ⌘ ⌘ ⌘ ⌘

God I am not sure what is going on with me but I am so scared. I am too weak to get up. Please don't let me die right here. Please help me.

⌘ ⌘ ⌘ ⌘ ⌘ ⌘ ⌘ ⌘ ⌘ ⌘ ⌘ ⌘

I could see my husband sleeping in bed, but I could not call his name loud enough for him to hear me. Eventually the dizziness subsided and I felt strong enough to crawl back to bed. The next morning, I told Randy what had happened. He immediately took me to the emergency room. From there I made an appointment to see my own doctor. She determined that all the stress of the last several years were starting to pile up: managing a hotel through three major hurricanes, a son who was constantly in trouble, a teenage daughter with a baby, combining households, getting married, ongoing arguing between the children, another daughter who was starting to rebel, and a dog. Any one of these would be enough to cause a person to feel overwhelmed, but combine them all and it adds up to a relapse of depression and anxiety. The increase in anxiety coupled with the lack of sleep due to insomnia caused my heart to race which resulted in me passing out on the bathroom floor. She suggested I take time to relax. She placed me on medical leave and prescribed a new antidepressant as well as prescription sleep aid. I had worked very hard to get off of antidepressants several years earlier. I felt so defeated to be told that I needed them again.

> *She prescribed an antideppresant and a prescription sleep aid ... here we go again!*

As the months passed, things continued to spin out of control. I left the job that I had held for over 10 years. Later, Randy lost the job that he had for nearly as long. We had a car repossessed. We lost our house. Without those well-paying jobs we knew we would not be able afford a house large enough for all of us. We could not agree upon a solution. Our family broke apart. We opted to put our children ahead of our marriage. My son had already moved out, but we had three other children and a grandchild at home. Randy moved into an apartment with his son and I moved in to an apartment with my daughters and grandson in the same apartment complex. Somehow we had convinced ourselves that this was the best solution. Although we were not officially separated, living apart had the same effect. We continued to grow apart. I was sure that our marriage was ending. I was so hurt and frustrated. At one point I researched the fastest and easiest way to file for divorce. I even went so far as to start filling out the paperwork, but it just felt so wrong. *How has this happened? How have did we get to this point?*

⌘ ⌘ ⌘ ⌘ ⌘ ⌘ ⌘ ⌘ ⌘ ⌘ ⌘ ⌘

God please help us. I don't want to be divorced again. I know this is not Your will. I love him. There has to be a way to work this out.

⌘ ⌘ ⌘ ⌘ ⌘ ⌘ ⌘ ⌘ ⌘ ⌘ ⌘ ⌘

We were not quite sure how we were going to do it but we made a commitment to make our marriage work.

Much like we had kept our families separate, we had also kept our faith separate. We were both Christians. We had talked about our faith, but were never active in it. Other than occasionally at the dinner table, we had never really even prayed together. We decided to attend church together. It was the best thing that we could have done. We had chosen a church that was focused on putting Christ at the center of everything in life. It seemed that each message was tailor made to help us strengthen our marriage. We immediately began to see so many things that we had done wrong. We decided that we needed to put Jesus first in our lives, then our marriage, and together we could make the best decisions regarding the rest of the family. We began to make better decisions. We even learned how to discuss how we had hurt each other in the past. We were able to forgive each other and repair much of the damage that had been done. Of course problems didn't disappear and our life together was far from perfect. We still had a lot of challenges as all married couples do, but we were building a strong foundation. Just knowing that divorce was no longer an option in either of our hearts gave us both the determination to keep fighting.

We joined the church and started to attend on a regular basis. Although this was a very large church, once we began to serve and volunteer on a regular basis we felt connected and at home—we belonged. I had never had such a connection with a church in my whole life. Up to this point, our faith had always been something that we considered private. Now we just wanted to shout to the world how the love Jesus had saved us. Although we had both been baptized as children, we decided we needed to publicly declare our faith as adults. We were baptized together on September 11, 2011 just three days after our fourth anniversary. To us we were not only recommitting our individual lives to Christ, we were also committing our marriage to Christ as well.

⌘ ⌘ ⌘ ⌘ ⌘ ⌘ ⌘ ⌘ ⌘ ⌘ ⌘ ⌘

Thank you Lord for our salvation.
Thank you for saving our marriage.

Our Public Declaration of Faith

Our stronger faith was put to the test many times in the coming years. My children continued to make life choices that were not conducive to their health and well-being. We tried to help and support them when we could, but mostly we had to leave them to make their own mistakes. As a mother that was difficult for me. I wanted to fix it. I wanted to make them do what was necessary to improve their lives. I wanted to demand that they do better. Seeing my children struggle was so hard for me and I carried so much guilt. I was sure that the decisions I had made were what had caused them to get so far off track. This meant I was willing to do anything I could to help them. I prayed for God's protection over them. I pleaded with Him to save them.

Chapter Fifteen

Destination: Glory

"Hey Honey?" I heard my husband calling to me from the bedroom.

"Yes, dear?" I look up and smile as he enters the room. *He's so handsome.*

"Did you know that there is a job fair at our church today?" he asks.

"Oh, I think I remember hearing something about it," I say as I turn away completely uninterested. He can sense that I am not enthusiastic about the idea.

"There are supposed to some good employers there. I really wish that I could go. I guess you probably won't go," he sighed.

I wasn't sure if he was disappointed that he was not going or because he felt that I wouldn't. *How dare he sigh at me! How does he know that I'm not going? Is he insinuating that I am lazy? I don't even have anything to wear. I might go. I hate when he thinks he knows me so well.* He kissed me goodbye and headed out the door. The more I sat there thinking about the job fair, the more I felt I should go. I have to admit, one of the main reasons I decided to go was to prove my husband wrong. I wanted to prove that he didn't know me as well as he thought. I wanted to prove that I was not lazy. I put on my best professional outfit and gathered the most recent copies of my resumé and headed out the door. I arrived at the church and headed into the job fair. *There are so many people here!* I didn't really feel that I had make any real connections for a job, but I was happy that I had gotten out of the house.

Over the past few years Randy had been able to find a stable job. He wasn't sure if it was the right job for him, but it was stable. I had not been so fortunate. I had worked for the last few years as an independent insurance agent but the work and pay were sporadic and unpredictable and there were no benefits. I had briefly returned to the hospitality industry, but left again after I found a position in Human Resources. Now after a recent foot and ankle surgery I had returned to work to find that my position had been given away and my hours had been reduced from full-time to part-time. I understood why Randy wanted me to go to the job fair. Even though the experience was very uplifting it had not resulted in a job. Not having an adequate job was difficult. I felt like I wasn't contributing enough to the household. I knew that there was a job—the right job—out there for me, I was just having trouble finding it. I was trying not to worry about it. I was trying to have faith that it would all work out. I knew that God had a plan for me.

My oldest daughter now had two little boys. When we felt that her choices were putting her sons in jeopardy, we stepped in and took temporary custody of them. At times she lived with us as well, but most of the time we were raising her children. The added responsibility put a greater strain on our finances. This strain on finances caused a lot of stress in our marriage. Again, the stronger foundation we had built gave us the ability to work through this strain. It was not always easy, and frankly many times it was extremely hard, but we were able to pull through each and every time.

I no longer felt the need to take antidepressants but I could still occasionally feel the downward tug of depression. When those times came I was able to pray my way through it. I was so thankful to have this option. Prayer brought to me a sense of peace and calm that even with medication I had not been able to maintain before. I found that the hopelessness and despair of depression was not able to thrive in the face of prayer. Prayer is hope.

The despair of depression was not able to thrive in the face of prayer.

Months after the job fair I received a call from one of the employers I had applied with. It was a local prayer ministry. They had a position open and wanted me to come in for an interview. I was nervous. I had no idea what to expect, but I went to the interview anyway. I was called to interview for one position, but during the course of the interview was offered another position. I accepted the job as a receptionist. I had no idea at the time that the decision to take that job would impact the lives of my family in ways that I could not even begin to imagine. As it turned out, this ministry was focused on prayer for healing—complete healing.

As the receptionist I was in the middle of everything that happened. I would answer calls and transfer them to prayer partners for prayer. Then many times I was able to hear each person as they were prayed for. I started to notice the number of women who were calling distressed about problems that their adult children were having. I was astonished by the number of calls we received about this. Finally, I had to admit that perhaps God was trying to send me a message through these calls. Each time I would lean in to hear the prayers that were being said. Eventually I started to say the prayers as they were being said over the phone. Each time the prayer partner would lead the mother in a prayer to place her adult children on the altar of Jesus Christ. The mother would promise to leave them there and let God work on healing them. I promised too. Then they would pray against false responsibility. The mother would ask for God to forgive her for any wrong choices she made while raising her children. I asked too. She would then relinquish any current responsibility for wrong choices her adult child was making. I let it go too. The freedom that I gained walking through those prayers over and over again was nothing short of miraculous.

When I started work at the ministry, the head of the ministry was out of the country. She returned a couple of weeks after I started. I knew she would be coming in to meet me and I was so nervous. I had no idea what to think. She had been referred to as a healing evangelist. All of this was very new to me. The only evangelist I was familiar with were the ones on TV and quite frankly, they scared me. I did know that everyone in the ministry loved and respected her. As she walked in I was immediately put at ease. She came over and introduced herself and said, "I heard you have been having some pain."

What? How did she now that? She had never met me until now. God must have told her! Actually it was our Office Manager that told her but still, she was there to help.

"Yes, ma'am but it's okay. It's no too bad right now," I tell her.

The truth is I had been having a great deal of pain in my joints and bones for quite so long I couldn't remember not having it. Some days were better than others. She insisted that any pain was too much and offered to pray for me. I accepted. She held my hands and said a very simple prayer. She lightly touched the areas that were hurting and commanded the pain to go away and it did. I was completely pain free! It's amazing how you don't realize how much pain you have been living with until it is completely gone. Then she gently touched my shoulders and looked me right in the eyes and said, "I know that you have a lot going on in your life right now. I understand that you are raising grandchildren. You have to do everything that it involves on a daily basis, but you do not have to carry the stress associated with it. Give the stress to God and move on with your life." She smiled and gave me a hug.

Her words have never left me. The idea that we don't have to carry the stress of daily life was so simple but so foreign to me. My whole life I had been told that life was stressful. That's just how it is. Motherhood is stressful. That's just how it is. We just have to deal with it. She was saying that we don't. God says we don't. I could literally feel the joy that had lost so long ago filtering back through my body. It felt like sunshine. I felt like my life was shifting from shades of gray to the colors of the rainbow. All of the situations in my life had remained the same but shifting the stress of making them change from me to God made a difference in an instant. Each day I learned more and more about healing. Each time I learned something new I was set free of something that had been holding me back. I could certainly get used to this.

> *Shifting the stress of making things change from me to God made a difference in an instant.*

The next year, Randy and I made the decision to become ordained ministers through this ministry. We didn't completely understand at the time, but we knew that God had plans for us. In preparation for this ordination we had to read and study a lot of material. During this course of study, I was learning how to lead people through a prayer of forgiveness. By going through the prayer I was able to forgive a lot of people in my life. I had heard one of the prayer partners tell someone on the phone if they weren't sure if they needed to forgive someone then they should just ask God. I wanted to make sure I was free from unforgiveness so I prayed and asked God.

⌘ ⌘ ⌘ ⌘ ⌘ ⌘ ⌘ ⌘ ⌘ ⌘ ⌘ ⌘

God is there anyone else that I needed to forgive? Please show me if there is anyone else that I am holding a grudge against.

⌘ ⌘ ⌘ ⌘ ⌘ ⌘ ⌘ ⌘ ⌘ ⌘ ⌘ ⌘

He answered, "YOU."

I was confused. *Me? Yes, me ... is there anyone else that I need to forgive.*

Then He clearly replied, "You need to forgive yourself."

That simple commandment shook me to the core, but I realized He was so right. I had made an effort to let go of so many things, really big things, that others had done to cause me so much pain but I had not even considered what I was doing to myself.

For some reason, to forgive others was easier than forgiving myself. It was almost like I felt like I should have known better. As hard as it was, I did it. I forgave myself for every mistake that I had made as a mother. I knew I would never have done anything to intentionally hurt my children. I knew that I tried to do what was best for them. Forgiving myself erased any leftover guilt that had been lingering in my heart. It gave me the ability to make decisions based on God's will and not based on trying to make up for things that I felt I had done wrong in the past. I was able to completely let go of control over my children's lives and actions and truly trust God to heal them. He has been faithful.

Glory: (n) a state of grandeur, magnificence; praise, prestige, honor.

I have reached a place of glory in my life. I have peace and I have found true happiness. My family is being restored. God is doing His part and I am working hard to do my part. My part is mostly to stay out of His way and trust Him to do what He has said He will do. My part has been to help raise my three grandsons as He heals and restores my daughter. My part has been to provide unconditional love and prayer support as they heal and learn to trust and follow Him. To be at this place in my life represents victory; joyful, glorious victory. *Thank you Jesus!*

All Smiles as We Begin to Heal

Conclusion

"**M**eme? Can someone mess up the plan that God has for their life?" my grandson asks as I tuck him into bed.

I had just prayed with him and at the end I always thank God for the plans that He has for his life. I guess it got him to thinking. *Wow. That's a good question. He's only eight years old. Where does he come up with these questions?* I think about it for a moment. I am confident that I know the answer, but I am trying to figure out how to best explain it to him.

"No," I explain, "You cannot mess up the plan. You can choose to not follow the plan, but it will still be there."

He looks confused.

"It's like riding your bike. Think of the sidewalk as God's plan. You can choose to stay on the sidewalk and go in the direction that God tells you or you can decide to do something different. You can turn off into the grass. You can get off the sidewalk and go over the curb. It may be more dangerous. You may fall down and you may get hurt. Once you have had enough, the sidewalk is still there and you can get back on it and go where you are supposed to go. Does that make sense?" I try to gage by his expression if he is comprehending any of what I had just said.

"I get it!" he says, "I know what you are saying. Sometimes you tell me stuff and I don't get it, but this time I get it."

I am just as happy as he is. My love for this kid fills my whole heart.

"Thank you Meme. I love you. I don't know what I would do without you. Good night," and he looks me right in the eyes while he pats my hand.

I plant kisses on his face and make sure he's all tucked in. I check on his two little brothers and they are sleeping peacefully. As I leave the room I hear him say, "Thank you God for my Meme. Thank you from my brothers too."

Of course, I cried.

⌘ ⌘ ⌘ ⌘ ⌘ ⌘ ⌘ ⌘ ⌘ ⌘ ⌘ ⌘

Thank you God for the do over. Thank you for the unexpected opportunity to use the wisdom you have given me to help raise these babies. Thank you.

⌘ ⌘ ⌘ ⌘ ⌘ ⌘ ⌘ ⌘ ⌘ ⌘ ⌘ ⌘

My journey through motherhood has been an eventful one. It has been filled with unexpected blessings, heartaches, surprises, and joy. At first glance it seems so far from the picture that I had in my head before I started off. On closer examination I realize that it is not. I always wanted five kids. I had three of my own and when I married Randy I got the other two. I wanted to be the best mom. I was the very best that I could be. I wanted to be the mom that all kids wanted to have. I was able to love and nurture a lot of children in addition to my own. I gave them the love and support they needed at the time, that is something I know for sure they wanted. I was caring and loving. I gave and still give an abundance of hugs and kisses. I sing. I even dance. I am an amazing cook and on occasion my house can be very clean. My color palette has changed a bit, but my home is colorful and bright.

God even blessed me with the opportunity to experience each of the careers that I had dreamed of. When my daughters wanted to dance I became ballerina mom. That one time when the laundry basket got too close to the water heater in the laundry room I was fireman mom. When dealing with all the various childhood illnesses I was nurse mom with an occasional promotion to doctor mom. Lawyer mom was needed to explain the full meaning of my rules and regulations and how they had been broken. At homework time I was teacher mom. Juggling finances I needed to be accountant mom. Trying to figure out who broke my lamp I was forensic scientist mom. Identifying the mystery substance in the refrigerator called for microbiologist mom. Finally, when relaying the play by play of my son's fabulous catch in his little league game, I got to be sports commentator mom.

I have even made peace with the verse that haunted me for so long. *She is clothed with strength and dignity* (I am!); *she can laugh at the days to come* (I can!). *She speaks with wisdom* (God has given me so much), *and faithful instruction is on her tongue* (I am here to speak the love and power of Jesus). *She watches over the affairs of her household* (I do in union with my dear husband) *and does not eat the bread of idleness* (Not always, but I did just write a book and that's something)! *Her children arise and call her blessed* (They do); *her husband also, and he praises her* (The love and support of my husband is one of my most treasured gifts): *"Many women do noble things, but you surpass them all"* (Proverbs 31:25-29).

For so many years I worried. I carried guilt. I thought I had done so much damage and caused so much pain. Recently I asked my adult children what they remembered most about their childhood and me as their mother. I braced myself to hear about the sadness or me yelling or working too many hours. I was not all prepared for what I actually heard. My son remembers playing sports. He remembers me always being there are cheering him on. He remembers me as a sports mom. My oldest daughter remembers the musical group *Hootie and the Blowfish*. She remembers their CD playing and us singing and dancing around the house. She remembers me as a fun mom. My youngest daughter remembers feeling loved and protected. She remembers sitting in my lap and being held. She remembers me as a nurturing mom. I tell you that to say this: many times the things that you are worrying about and holding onto are only real to you.

Even if your children do have unpleasant memories from childhood, how is worrying and stressing about it now going to help the situation? It isn't. So, stop it. Give yourself a break. You deserve it. If you are reading this book, your story is not over. Your journey has not ended. Pick your bike up. Put on your helmet. Peddle towards glory and enjoy your ride.

A New Set of Noisemakers

Donya Russell is a motivational speaker who uses the fresh revelation God has given her through life experiences to see women healed and made whole through His power and love. With wit and humor, her approach is authentic—real and honest—and causes us to find the divine right in the middle of all things ordinary.

Let's Connect!

- Invite Donya to speak.
- Follow Donya on facebook.
- Learn more!

donyarussell.com